American Society of Missiology Series, No. 4

MEANING
ACROSS
CULTURES

Eugene A. Nida

William D. Reyburn

ORBIS BOOKS
Maryknoll, New York 10545

The American Society of Missiology Series, in collaboration with Orbis Books, seeks to publish scholarly works of high merit and wide interest on numerous aspects of missiology—the study of mission. Able presentations on new and creative approaches to the practice and understanding of mission will receive close attention.

The Catholic Foreign Mission Society of America (Maryknoll) recruits and trains people for overseas missionary service. Through Orbis Books Maryknoll aims to foster the international dialogue that is essential to mission. The books published, however, reflect the opinions of their authors and are not meant to represent the official position of the society.

Published by Orbis Books, Maryknoll, NY 10545
in collaboration with the American Society of Missiology

Manuscript Editor: William E. Jerman

Library of Congress Cataloging in Publication Data
Nida, Eugene Albert, 1914-
    Meaning across cultures.

    (American Society of Missiology series; no. 4)
    Bibliography: p.
    Includes index.
    1. Bible—Translating. 2. Communication.
3. Religion and culture. I. Reyburn, William
David. II. Title. III. Series.
BS449.N53   220.5   81-38374
ISBN 0-88344-326-0 (bpk.)   AACR2

Contents

Preface to the Series

The purpose of the ASM Series is to publish, without regard for disciplinary, national, or denominational boundaries, scholarly works of high quality and wide interest on missiological themes from the entire spectrum of scholarly pursuits, e.g., theology, history, anthropology, sociology, linguistics, health, education, art, political science, economics, and development, to articulate but a partial list. Always the focus will be on Christian mission.

By "mission" in this context is meant a cross-cultural passage over the boundary between faith in Jesus Christ and its absence. In this understanding of mission, the basic functions of Christian proclamation, dialogue, witness, service, fellowship, worship, and nurture are of special concern. How does the transition from one cultural context to another influence the shape and interaction of these dynamic functions?

Missiologists know that they need the other disciplines. And other disciplines, we dare to suggest, need missiology, perhaps more than they sometimes realize. Neither the insider's nor the outsider's view is complete in itself. The world Christian mission has through two millennia amassed a rich and well-documented body of experience to share with other disciplines.

Interaction will be the hallmark of this Series. It desires to be a channel for talking to one another instead of about one another. Secular scholars and church-related missiologists have too long engaged in a sterile venting of feelings about one another, often lacking in full evidence. Ignorance of and indifference to one another's work has been no less harmful to good scholarship.

We express our warm thanks to various mission agencies whose financial contributions enabled leaders of vision in the ASM to launch this new venture. The future of the ASM series will, we feel sure, fully justify their confidence and support.

William J. Danker, Chairperson
ASM Series Editorial Committee

Preface

Two developments have prompted the preparation of this volume, *Meaning Across Cultures*. One is the increasingly recognized need for some practical guide to help people understand how misconceptions can arise because of differing cultural backgrounds, especially as these relate to many crucial differences between the cultural preconceptions and values of biblical times and those of our own day. The second is the need for an exposition of the principles of communication that may guide one's judgment as to the validity of various types of adaptation and restructuring that occur in many present-day translations of the Bible.

In an effort to avoid traditional and often meaningless word-for-word renderings of the Scriptures, some translators have so altered the linguistic form as to seriously distort the meaning of the text and have so transposed the cultural content as to undermine the significance of the historical setting. And so it becomes necessary to define and describe the principles that govern faithfulness and accuracy in intercultural communication.

The special emphasis of this volume is not upon translation techniques, but upon those basic differences of ideas and attitudes that are so fundamental to any attempt to understand a message produced by persons of a significantly diverse culture. The focus of attention is, therefore, directed not so much to isolated words as to those objects and events in the Scriptures that have quite distinct meanings from what they have in many receptor cultures. Accordingly, special consideration is given to the problems involved in providing in marginal notes and appendices the supplementary information essential for a satisfactory understanding of the biblical message.

The principles in question are treated in terms of the underlying theory of communication, presented primarily in chapters 2 and 3. This is then followed in chapters 4 and 5 by an analysis of the implications of these principles for matters of form and content. A number of practical implications and applications are discussed in chapters 6 and 7.

1
Meaning Across Cultures:
An Introduction

All communication across cultures involves problems of meaning, for the words of any language have meaning only in terms of the ideas, values, and circumstances of concrete human lives. In English we can say that "God forgives," even though we do not really understand what the particles *for* and *give* in the word *forgive* have to do with the act of forgiving. But in one of the languages of central New Guinea one can speak of God's forgiveness only by saying, "God doesn't hang up jawbones." In English we "love with the heart," but in many languages in West Africa one must "love with the liver." Strangely enough we speak of the larynx as "Adam's apple," while the Uduks of the Sudan call it "the thing that loves beer."

In one language of New Guinea spoken by persons who have no acquaintance with sheep but who prize very much their carefully tended pigs, a Bible translator proposed substituting "pig-herder" for "shepherd." Such an adjustment would obviously create serious problems because pigs are regarded as unclean animals in the Bible. This type of cultural adaptation can be dismissed as being poorly conceived, but how is one to respond to the insistence of a professor of theology who contends that a dynamic equivalent translation of the Old Testament phrase "thus saith the Lord" would have to be "I just had an important idea"? In both instances most readers would emphatically reject such suggestions for adjustment, but what are the reasons for rejection?

When the languages involved belong to the same language family and are part of a closely related set of cultures—as, for example, in the case of English and German—the problems are not too great, even though in English we have no satisfactory equivalent for *Gesundheit* spoken when a person sneezes, or for *gute Speise* spoken at the beginning of a meal. But when languages are of different language families and involve wide differences of culture—for example, English and Zulu—the difficulties of comprehension increase by almost geometric proportion. And if one adds to these problems certain differences in time, as between modern English and ancient Hebrew, the complications can be enormous.

The communication of meaning across cultures always requires certain adjustments in the form of the message if the content is to be accurately and faithfully transmitted, for strictly word-for-word renderings inevitably tend

1

to distort the meaning of the source-language message. But how far can one go in making such adjustments?

The traditional tendency to retain so many of the figures of speech and the cultural symbols of biblical life and times does undoubtedly produce serious misunderstanding, especially if the Bibles that contain such expressions have no accompanying marginal helps or adaptations enabling the reader to make some sense out of the seemingly anomalous expressions. In fact, difficulties arising out of differences of culture constitute the most serious problems for translators and have produced the most far-reaching misunderstandings among readers. A literal rendering of Romans 14:7, "no man lives unto himself and no man dies unto himself," has been interpreted by many Africans as being a direct confirmation of the efficacy of black magic, because death is almost never regarded as "natural" but is thought to result from the malevolent influence of witchcraft.

In many instances mistakes in comprehending a biblical text are not too serious, because no important theological issue is at stake. West Africans, for example, may read in a translation of the Bible in their mother tongue that a tax collector "beat his breast" as a sign of his repentance. This might seem strange indeed to West Africans in whose own language the idiom "to beat the breast" can only mean to take pride in one's accomplishment. To indicate repentance one should say "he beat his head."

This type of misunderstanding is not especially grave, but there are many instances when failure to deal satisfactorily with some of the basic cultural problems in communication has led to confusion. In one language a term for "reconciliation" was used for a number of years before missionaries discovered that the cultural practice to which it referred differed from biblical reconciliation in one very crucial aspect. In the local culture the use of this term immediately suggested that the persons who took the initiative in the act of reconciliation were admitting their own guilt in causing the initial rupture in relations. Such a term was completely misleading in speaking about God's attempts to reconcile human beings to himself.

In the case of "beating the breast," one may be able to employ a parallel expression "to beat the head." In treating the problem posed by the term for "reconciliation," one must either (1) find another term that does not have the implication of guilt for the initiating party, or (2) construct some phrase that will describe the essential elements of reconciliation in an unambiguous manner. But most problems that involve cultural differences are much more complex: they involve conflicting values attached to the same objects.

For example, in the Orient the "dragon" is not regarded as a threatening animal, symbolic of overwhelming evil power, as in the Book of Revelation; rather, the dragon suggests good luck and fortune. Is one to change the symbol of "dragon" to fit Oriental concepts? Or what should be done with the "white robes" of the saints in Korea where white is a symbol of mourning, not of purity? Furthermore, the concept of making robes white by "washing them in the blood of the Lamb" is almost incomprehensible in many languages; as one person in the Philippines tried to explain, "The blood of the Lamb must not have been red."

Misunderstandings frequently arise out of seemingly quite unimportant details. For example, in a literal translation of John 6:58, "the bread that your ancestors ate, and then died" may imply that the bread must have been poisonous and therefore caused death. Or in John 2:4 the use of "woman" in addressing Mary can only be understood in some languages as meaning "wife." Among some peoples of Southeast Asia, Revelation 3:20 can be badly misconstrued because "knocking on doors" is understood to be a signal from a lover who wants his girl friend to meet him at some rendezvous. But for the Bazanaki people of East Africa this same phrase would imply that Jesus was a thief because only thieves knock on doors (to determine if there is anyone in the house); honest persons call out the names of those inside, and by doing so they identify themselves.

Most persons would consider these problems of translation minor difficulties that can readily be overcome with judicious adjustments of detail. In place of "woman" in John 2:4 one could use "mother" (as in the New English Bible), and in Revelation 3:20 one may employ "call" rather than "knock." But how is one to treat the contention of some scholars that the persons who are spoken of in the Bible as "demon possessed" were only "mentally distressed"? Some scholars insist that the demoniac's use of the name "Legion" (Mark 5:9) indicates that he merely suffered an "identity crisis" and that therefore this fact should be incorporated into the text. One German theologian recently proposed that the term *Gott* ("God") should be eliminated from the Bible and *Wirklichkeit* ("reality") be substituted for it. In Romans 1:7 we would then read, "May Reality, our Father, and the Lord Jesus Christ give you grace and peace." This type of proposal is unsatisfactory, but on what grounds?

How is it that some adjustments seem reasonable and others are quite unacceptable? If certain changes can be introduced, why not any and all changes? Are there any limits in such a procedure?

If one is translating Hindu theosophical texts or Buddhist meditative discourses, the need for careful reflection of cultural differences is not so great, because these texts do not take history so seriously. But the biblical texts do take history seriously—in fact, extremely so, for it is God's entrance into history, either in the history of his people or the incarnation of his Son, that is the crucial element of the biblical account. And it is precisely for this reason that one must be seriously concerned with problems of changes in form so that the content may be both clear and faithful to the original historical setting.

Some changes are clearly obligatory. For example, in the transliteration of proper names, one must adjust to the sounds of the receptor language. One cannot expect English readers of the Bible to pronounce the various Hebrew gutturals. It is also obvious that certain adjustments must be made in the grammatical categories and forms of words. Hebrew verbs are predominantly aspectual—that is, they primarily indicate completed as distinguished from uncompleted action—whereas English verbs customarily express various distinctions in tense. These differences clearly require some adjustments. Similarly, long involved sentences in the Greek New Testament need to be broken up into smaller units if the meaning of the original is to be communicated effectively in a language such as English. Likewise, idioms such as "bowels of mercy," "circumcised of heart," and "gird up the loins of the mind" require some adaptations if they are to be anything other than confusing sequences of terms.

In some instances it may be necessary to invert the contents of individual verses; but if so, then why not change the order of the paragraphs? Why, for example, follow the order of the narrative of the Prodigal Son when the story might be more effectively told by starting the young man out in the pigpen and then providing the background information by means of flashbacks? Why is it that some translators do not hesitate to change "white as snow" to "very, very white" (if snow may not be known in the culture), but do not want to translate "the uncircumcision" and "the circumcision" by "Gentiles" and "Jews," respectively, as in Romans 3:30, even though verse 29 indicates clearly what is meant?

In cultures in which there is no practice of anointing, certain references to anointing are translated by terms meaning "to commission" or "to designate for a task"; but in societies that do not practice sacrifice, translators insist upon finding some way to describe such religious activities, despite their strange content. But why should such a distinction be made? Many translators do not hesitate to substitute "hyenas" for "wolves" in the expression "wolves in sheep's clothing," but they do not believe that "sheep" should be changed to "goats," even though in the local culture goats are highly prized and sheep are neglected scavengers.

To find adequate answers to the problems that translators face, not only in the practical phases of working out acceptable solutions to differences of cultural content and values, but also in providing a well-grounded defense for what has been done, one must have more than a series of "rules of thumb" that seem acceptable and helpful. Nothing less than a thorough analysis of all the major factors involved in the communication of messages can provide the necessary foundation for fully adequate principles and procedures of adjustment. Such an analysis inevitably requires a consideration of the theory of communication, as applied specifically to translating, because anything short of such a detailed study tends to raise far more questions than it resolves.

2
What Communicating Means

In analyzing translation one must begin with a satisfactory model of communication. By means of such a model one can describe the principal factors and relations that enter into the communication of a message in the source language. What is required is something far more sophisticated than merely ready answers to "who said what to whom under what circumstances and for what purposes?" This shorthand summary of some of the basic elements in exegesis can be useful, but it is not enough for a thorough study of the many complicating factors in communication.

Communication Model

In any analysis of translating, the point of departure must be the original communication. This means beginning with three essential elements of the communication: the source (S), the message (M), and the receptor (R), which may be diagrammatically represented as follows:

$$S \rightarrow M \rightarrow R$$

Without these three basic elements there is simply no communication.

In this chapter the emphasis is upon communication within a single language ("intralingual communication"); in Chapter 3 the communication model is extended to include interlingual communication—in other words, translating.

In order to understand a message produced by a source, it is important to know as much as possible about the source; inevitably both the form and the content of a message that the source encodes have been determined by many factors relating to the source's own personality and experience. In general, this information can be divided into two types: (1) general background (e.g., education, social status, occupation, religious affiliation) and (2) linguistic background (e.g., mother tongue, language of education, literary training, sources of allusions and quotations). To understand the quotations in the Pauline letters it is important to know that most of them are based on the Septuagint rather than on the Hebrew text. This does not mean that Paul was unacquainted with the Hebrew text, but only that he did not hesitate to quote the Greek translation, especially at those points where it served his special purposes.

In describing the message, it is essential to distinguish two important elements: (1) the form and (2) the content. The form consists in all the formal features, starting with the sounds and proceeding to the level of literary genre. Many of the formal features of any message are obligatory—that is, they are imposed by the nature of the language itself, without the speaker's necessarily thinking consciously of them as part of the message. These features include the sounds represented in the alphabet, the forms of the words, the syntax of the sentences, and many of the features of the discourse (e.g., the use of active versus passive, the sequence of clauses). All such features are obligatory in that they are largely dictated by the formal requirements of the language itself. Not all formal features, however, are determined by the language structure. Many of them are optional—for example, the order of ideas in expository discourse, the choice of literary forms (e.g., parable, allegory, proverb), and the employment of certain rhetorical devices (e.g., rhetorical questions, chiasmus, parallelism, double negatives for emphasis).

The content of any message is derived principally from two different sets of relations: (1) the relation of verbal symbols to one another (the "formal meaning," involving both syntactic and rhetorical levels), and (2) the relation of verbal symbols to features of the nonlinguistic world (the "referential meaning"). In general, it is this latter type of meaning to which one most often refers in speaking of the meaning of any message. In fact when speaking about the message of the Bible, the term "meaning" is often used on at least two quite different levels: (1) the immediate meaning of a specific passage and (2) the higher, or theological, significance of the passage. Hence, the meaning of passages about the crucifixion of Jesus is sometimes discussed in terms of the actual events described, but more often in terms of the symbolic or metaphysical importance of this crucial event in "salvation history."

Except where otherwise noted, referential meaning is restricted in this analysis to the first level of meaning because this is the level of meaning that is of primary importance for Bible translators. This does not imply any depreciation of higher levels of meaning. It is only that the higher levels are basically secondary, in the sense of being built upon the first level.

This first level of meaning, consisting of both formal and referential relations, involves two different aspects: cognitive and emotive. The cognitive aspect is the conceptual understanding of the relations between the verbal symbols themselves and between these and the nonlinguistic (practical world) objects, events, and abstracts, for which they stand. The emotive aspect involves the manner in which those who participate in the communication event react emotionally to the formal and referential aspects of the message.

The formal features themselves involve both cognitive and emotive elements. The formal order of ideas, reflecting certain logical relations (e.g., cause and effect, reason and result, generic and specific), are purely cognitive, but the manner in which the formal elements are arranged may produce marked differences in emotive reactions. The balance of lines, the rhythmic arrangements of words, the parallelism of thought may have a very pleasing form, irrespective of the content. When there is a particularly effective combination of cognitive and emotive aspects of both the form and the content, one may be assured that this is a truly literary production, as in chapter 13 of 1 Corinthians, for example.

In dealing with referential meaning, it is essential to make certain important distinctions related to the roles of the participants. For example, the meaning that a source wishes to convey may be stated as the "intent." Whether the intent is properly communicated or not may be quite another matter. Furthermore, a source may have had an intent that is quite different from the apparent content of the message. This is particularly true of irony, in which the evident intent contrasts purposely with the usual meaning of such a message. One must also reckon with the fact that no two receptors are ever likely to comprehend and respond to a message in identically the same way. This means that absolute communication is never possible, for no two individuals ever share completely the same linguistic and cultural backgrounds.

In comparing the intentions of a source with the understanding of a receptor, one must not expect to find identity. In general, however, the two are close enough to be culturally functional, and this is what ultimately counts.

Some analysts of meaning wish to add to the intention of the source and the meaning for the receptor a third kind of participant meaning: the "theoretical norm"—that is, how a particular message should be understood by persons within a particular language-culture context. Some might prefer to call this "theoretical norm" the "legal meaning" or the "ideal meaning."

Still other persons would like to include a "timeless meaning"—that is, a meaning of a message that would be unrelated to a specific time-space cultural setting. This has been called by some the "theological meaning" and by others the "hermeneutical meaning." But this is an issue that can concern us only after we have analyzed somewhat more fully some of the basic elements in communication between languages.

Multiple Levels of Meaning

All messages have a first level of meaning. This is the immediate (often called the "literal") meaning of a passage and one on which in most instances most persons can agree. There are of course passages that are ambiguous or obscure because we no longer know enough of the background to understand what is being talked about—for example, the necessity of being salted with fire (Mark 9:49). In some instances, there are purposeful ambiguities, reflecting the intention of the author, as when the Gospel of John (3:8) likens the Spirit to wind (using the Greek *pneuma*); but in most instances of intentional ambiguities, the context signals the play on words.

Intentional ambiguities can rarely be reproduced in a translation, and accordingly some marginal help is necessary if the reader is to understand the formal features involved. Ambiguities that result from the scholars' lack of understanding should likewise be identified. This is best done by means of marginal helps or supplementary lists because attempts to reproduce them in the translation do injustice to the original author who evidently had one or another meaning in mind and was not trying to be obscure. To expect the untrained reader to resolve such obscurities is fair neither to the reader nor to the original author.

In addition to a first level of meaning, many passages of Scripture have two or more higher levels. It is the very essence of a parable to contain both a first-level meaning—that is, an account of what happened in the illustrative story—and a second-level meaning, the "point" of the story. The story of the Lost Sheep (Luke 15:1–7) is not merely a narrative about a shepherd who left ninety-nine sheep in order to look for one lost sheep. It has a second-level meaning—namely, the attitude of God toward sinners. In fact this second-level meaning is the real point of the story.

Some parables may have several different levels or reveal multiple meanings on a higher level. The story of the Prodigal Son tells something about the penalties paid for sin, the egotism of self-righteousness, and the meaning of suffering love.

Allegories are narratives in which most or all of the individual details have some higher, or symbolic, level of meaning. But in allegories the double levels of meaning are generally quite obvious, and in many instances the relations are made quite specific.

For the most part, multiple levels of meaning are marked by certain formal features of a context. The symbolic meanings of the *words* "Adam" and "Eve" suggest that these names are something more than simply designations of a man and his wife. The lack of important historical details in the story of Cain and Abel may also be taken to indicate that these events have more than a single level of signification. In certain instances, special emphasis, indicated by unexpected repetitions, may carry meaning, as in the case of Ruth who is referred to as a Moabitess or from the land of Moab a total of eight times in the short book bearing her name. Some scholars have thought that this may be important in understanding the purpose behind the writing of the book—namely, as a defense of the Jews who had taken Moabite wives and were suffering from the strictures laid down by Ezra and Nehemiah.

In some instances, a first level of interpretation may be so unacceptable to some persons as to compel them to see only a higher level. This has often been true in the interpretation of the Song of Songs, in which the first-level meaning of sexual love is completely allegorized in terms of the relation of Christ to his church.

It is even possible to see some higher-level meaning in what is not said. For example, Luke's detailed treatment of the life and ministry of Paul seems to stop short of what one would expect to be the climax of the story—namely, the condemnation of Paul and his death. But this obviously did not fit Luke's purpose. At no place in his Gospel and the Acts of the Apostles does Luke indicate any direct condemnation of the Christian movement by Roman authorities. The fact that Luke ends his account of Paul by indicating that he was able to preach the Good News "with boldness and freedom," thus omitting entirely any mention of later developments, may be said to communicate something on a "higher level," without, of course, making it explicit.

Though the translator is not so immediately concerned with the higher levels of meaning as is the expositor or the preacher, he cannot properly undertake to translate any text without an awareness of these multiple levels of meaning.

Role of Receptors

No analysis of communication can be complete without a thorough study of the role of the receptors of a message. In the first place, it is important to know about their general background (e.g., their ethnic origins, religious beliefs, educational levels) as well as their linguistic background (e.g., their mother tongue, any supplementary language or languages, and in the case of the Bible the language in which the existing Scriptures were read). For example, for most Christians of the first century, the Scriptures were the Greek translation of the Old Testament, known as the Septuagint.

In some cases, it would be very useful if we knew who certain receptors were. Who, for example, was Theophilus, to whom Luke addressed his Gospel and the Acts of the Apostles? Was his name merely symbolic, "beloved by God"? Was he some government official to whom Luke was making his defense and explanation of Christianity? Was he a Christian or a pagan? Or is it possible that he was the one who underwrote the publication of these books (for ancient writings often did have a dedication to the publisher or benefactor)? The fact that we do not know who Theophilus was only highlights the importance of knowing to whom a message is specifically or generally directed. The reason for wanting to identify the receptors is that one can then judge more accurately the basis for the author's particular formulation of his message.

Normally, the receptors of any important message are likely to reflect differences in backgrounds, interests, and values. There are even two quite different theories as to receptors to whom the Epistle to the Galatians was directed. Paul seems to be unusually explicit in the analogy between Sarah and Hagar, on the one hand, and between Jerusalem and Sinai, on the other. But obviously the Judaizers among those receiving the letter would have had an interpretation of these analogies entirely different from the one that Paul had. Paul evidently assumed that all persons involved would know something about the Old Testament background to this illustration, but he could never have thought that they would necessarily all agree with him.

How receptors understand a message does not depend primarily upon their knowledge of the cultural or historical backgrounds involved, but upon their evaluation of these. Jehovah's Witnesses and Southern Baptists may have essentially similar objective information concerning certain biblical passages, but they put the information into very different conceptual structures, with the result that their interpretation of these passages is entirely different. The same was evidently true of the Pauline and the Judaizing parties in early Christianity. Understanding the message, therefore, consists in much more than mere possession of certain information. The message has meaning only in terms of certain all-embracing structures of thought, which include preeminently the basic presuppositions and tenets of the receptor culture or subculture. But these factors cannot be considered until some further attention has been given to the setting of the communication.

Setting of the Communication

The setting of communication (whether of spoken or written messages) consists of three factors: (1) time, (2) location, and (3) roles of the participants. The temporal factors are divided into three phases: (a) prior events that may influence the nature of the communication, (b) the actual time of the communication, and (c) the later events, including anything that is known about the response of the receptors to the communication. The importance of prior events is emphasized negatively in the difficulties that scholars encounter in trying to understand 2 Corinthians. If we only knew precisely what the events were that prompted Paul to write as he did, it would be so much easier to understand the message of this letter.

Some persons have thought that they could ascertain the response of the original receptors of Paul's letters by noting the ways in which these letters were interpreted by the early Christian Fathers. But most of the writings of the Fathers are dated some two to three hundred years after Paul's letters, and in some ways they are further removed in time than we are today, inasmuch as we possess a great deal of historical data that was not generally available to the Christian exegetes of the third and fourth centuries. What we need to know, and what in so many instances we do not know, is how receptors responded at the time. It is the lack of such information that so greatly impairs our ability to interpret some of the difficult passages of the Scriptures.

The factor of location has to do with the place in which a communication occurs. Under traditional circumstances, oral communication would imply that the source and receptors were in the same place. Today this is often not the case, because radio and television present unusual opportunities for displacement in both time and place. But in terms of biblical communication, scholars are very much interested in the location of communication. Was the Gospel of John, for example, written in Ephesus, and does it therefore reflect what is regarded as a typically "Ephesian view" of Jesus?

The differential roles of source and receptors are also important in understanding a communication. Is the relationship one of teacher to students, official to subjects, petitioner to king, or prophet to people? These reciprocally related roles are important in understanding and evaluating both content and form. The roles of Paul and Philemon are important in understanding the meaning of Paul's one strictly personal letter. If we only knew the roles of source and receptors of the Book of Ruth, a number of problems would be cleared up almost immediately.

Noise

To understand certain problems associated with communication one must reckon with the factor of noise—anything that disturbs the message during the process of transmission. This may consist of obvious external physical noise, which may prevent the receptors from hearing correctly or adequately. But it may also be psychological noise—for example, interference with the message because of preconceptions about what people think should have been said. This is apparently something of what happened when Paul was brought before the council (Acts 23:1-10). The Pharisees and Sadducees were so opposed to one another that they heard neither Paul nor each other.

Other forms of psychological noise may consist of inattention or distraction. It is also possible to treat the influence of literary forms upon the content of a message as being a kind of "literary noise," because the forms themselves tend to distort the uniqueness of the actual communication event by providing a limited number of molds into which the infinite variety of actual experience must be accommodated.

Errors that occur in the process of manuscript copying and recopying may be regarded as a form of "noise," inasmuch as these modifications can alter the content of the message over a period of time. The accidental mistakes of copyists are, however, relatively easy to detect, because they tend to occur in readily recognized contexts—for example, elimination of lines that end or begin with the same sequence of letters or words, substitution of forms that are better known or fit the context better, and substitution of letters that represent identical sounds (this is a familiar feature in manuscripts that are written down from dictation).

It is by no means so easy to detect the changes that occur because scribes undertook to "improve" the text—for example, by making parallel passages more consistent in wording, by deleting or altering expressions that seemed to contradict certain theological viewpoints, and by adding expressions that may have been only marginal notes in a prior manuscript. Such expressions were often incorporated into a later manuscript because they seemed appropriate or simply because a later scribe assumed that an earlier scribe had omitted them and tried to correct the mistake by putting the omitted words in the margin. All scribal modifications may be regarded as "psychological noise"—the unconscious errors resulted from inattention or distraction, and the conscious alterations involved modifications that were influenced by certain scribal assumptions about matters of textual consistency, theological content, or fidelity to tradition.

For the biblical scholar, however, the most important factor of noise has simply been the loss of background information through the centuries. The original authors and receptors shared much background information that made the message meaningful. A high percentage of this background data is no longer available to us, and accordingly there are many passages of Scripture that cannot be properly understood. This is not because these passages were meaningless or obscure when they were first written. In fact there is no evidence that any of the Scriptures were purposely written in the form of Delphic oracles or as Kabbalistic messages. The writers of the Bible had a message—and usually a very urgent one. Hence, there was no premium placed upon obscurity or ambiguity.

Our lack of information about the meaning of the original texts of the Scriptures is not, however, limited merely to data concerning historical events or cultural practices. There are many fine points of grammatical structure that cannot be clearly interpreted, simply because we do not know enough about the ancient languages to be able to state with certainty how to interpret certain grammatical structures. For example, we do not know in John 13:2 whether the Devil "had put into the heart of Judas the idea of betraying Jesus" or whether the Devil "had already decided that Judas would betray Jesus."

Furthermore, there are many words, especially in the Old Testament, that occur only once, and are not otherwise known. When the context is not clear, one cannot be certain what these words mean. In some instances, related words from other languages may give us some clues, but it is always dangerous to depend upon similar roots or stems, because they may have quite different meanings, even in closely related languages.

The Medium and the Channel

Because biblical materials are exclusively in written form, one tends to overlook some of the communication problems involved in the medium and the channel. The medium is the communication code—for example, words (oral or written), pictures, ritual events, or spontaneous acts that may show love, hate, joy, or the like. The channel is the means by which the message is transmitted—for example, in ancient times by word of mouth or written document, and in our day often by radio or television.

Within the Bible itself there is much that reflects oral tradition. This would be true not only of some parts of such books as Genesis, Joshua, and Judges, but undoubtedly occurs elsewhere, in far more instances that many persons imagine. It is also true that in the New Testament many of the accounts of Jesus were no doubt passed on in oral form long before they were committed to writing. As long as there were numerous eyewitnesses to the events, it may have seemed quite irrelevant to write down anything, particularly since so many early Christians apparently thought that Jesus would be returning very soon "to put his enemies under his feet."

One entire branch of biblical scholarship—namely, literary analysis—is dedicated primarily to the reconstruction of the earliest sources of the biblical texts. Uncovering the presumed levels of tradition, whether written or oral, is a complex task with many uncertainties, but it is important in trying to understand the meaning of many texts, especially in their earliest forms.

The translator of the Bible, however, is primarily concerned with the document as finally prepared by a particular author or authors. This is what the translator must translate. To understand certain aspects of the Gospel of Luke, it is useful to study the implications of the background documents or traditions, to which Luke himself alludes in his introduction (Luke 1:1–4), but of primary significance is the manner in which Luke himself interpreted this material, not how earlier sources may have regarded the data. These problems introduce matters that can, however, be adequately treated only after further consideration is given to some of the broader implications of communication theory.

In order to understand more fully some of the problems of communication, it is essential to recognize that any channel presents some basic deficiencies. Written communications are always deficient to the extent that they do not fully reflect all the significant contrasts that exist in the spoken language. Differences of phrase-final pauses and intonational contours normally mark important syntactic boundaries, but more often than not they are either lacking in written texts or are only imperfectly marked. In texts of ancient Greek these phonological contrasts were conspicuously absent, and, to make matters worse, words were even written together without spaces between them.

Written channels of communication have the advantage of seeming to preserve forms more carefully than do oral traditions, but manuscripts had to be copied by hand and the size of editions was extremely limited, thus requiring extensive copying and recopying if wide circulation of any message was to be obtained. Thus one can readily understand how literally thousands of minor differences could creep into the manuscript tradition of something as extensive as the New Testament.

There is not the same wealth of variant readings for the Old Testament, due to the particular history of the text, but there are at least five thousand different readings that have a significant bearing upon the meaning of the text. Furthermore, because of a lack of numerous so-called witnesses to the text (in comparison with the New Testament, of which the number of different manuscripts is almost overwhelming), it is often quite impossible to ascertain the form of the Old Testament text with any high degree of certainty.

Work of the United Bible Societies

The Greek New Testament (Third Edition) published by the United Bible Societies contains several thousand textual variants that are important for the understanding of the text. Furthermore, these have been classified as A, B, C, or D, depending upon the extent to which the reading in the text is to be regarded as reliable. The Nestle-Aland Greek Text, which contains the same critical text, has a different apparatus, in that it lists all significant variants regardless of whether they are meaningfully significant, but it lacks the classification as to textual reliability.

For the Old Testament, a committee for the Hebrew Old Testament Text Project spent ten years of work in reviewing more than five thousand textual variants in the Old Textament that involve meaningful differences and applied the same type of classification as to textual reliability. The five preliminary reports of the committee's findings have now been published. The first of five final reports is to be published in 1981 (first in French and then in English). These will contain all the relevant evidence from ancient Hebrew manuscripts, ancient versions, medieval rabbinic sources, and modern textual studies, together with full explanations as to the basis for the committee's decisions.

Cultural Presuppositions

Much of the referential meaning for the receptors of any message depends upon the cultural presuppositions of a particular society. The presuppositions are the underlying assumptions, beliefs, and ideas that are generally shared by persons, but are rarely if ever described or defined, simply because they seem so basic and obvious as not to require verbal formulation. Note, for example, the question posed by the disciples to Jesus in John 9:2, "Whose sin was it that caused this man to be born blind? His own or his parents?" The disciples never questioned the fact that sin must have been the underlying cause of such a misfortune: this was a basic presupposition. Jesus' response must have been quite a shock. Similarly, the account of creation, which speaks of dividing the waters above the firmament from the waters beneath it, is based on a worldview that assumed a kind of dome in the sky, on which the stars had their places and through the windows of which rain could pour down upon the earth.

These underlying presuppositions about world and life can be conveniently divided into five classes: (1) the physical earth and living beings, (2) history and destiny, (3) supernatural beings, (4) interpersonal relations, and (5) intellectual activity.

1. *The physical earth and human beings.* There seems little doubt that for people of biblical times creation was regarded as something that took place in seven periods of twenty-four hours each, thus providing not only an explanation of creation that was far less fanciful than the Babylonian myths, but also serving to sanctify the seventh day as a distinctive period of religiously prescribed cessation from work. Furthermore, the world was regarded as being populated by only those groups that had descended from Shem, Ham, and Japheth. Because the loss of blood accompanied the loss of vital force (as blood flowed out, so did the life of a person or animal), so "life was in the blood," and blood sacrifice became a means of symbolizing "life."

Living beings were also classifiable as clean and unclean, those which could be eaten and those which could not. The lists of clean and unclean animals and birds provide a few classificatory clues, such as chewing the cud and the cloven hoof, but there is no attempt to explain or to justify the distinction between clean and unclean animals and birds. It is simply assumed as one of the basic facts about nature, without which many other distinctions in life would have little or no meaning.

2. *History and destiny.* Presuppositions about history and destiny are important, not only in view of the concept of "the chosen people," but also in relation to the ideas of a future reign of God, an era of peace, the triumph of righteousness, all of which are unique as far as the ancient world is concerned.

The concept of a binding covenant, taken from the realm of interpersonal relations, is one of the dominant elements in Old Testament thought about God and God's people. It is in the light of this presupposition that the prophet can proclaim ultimate hope and victory despite an almost hopeless immediate future. Because of the covenant love of God, there must ultimately be a triumph for the people of God, a reign of peace, and a vindication of righteousness. But without the presuppositions that underlay such proclamations of the prophets, these words could only have seemed to the people like empty dreams of demented seers.

As for the ultimate destiny of individual human beings, the Bible contains two sets of presuppositions that seem to be contradictory and are never resolved explicitly. In the Old Testament death and the grave (often spoken of as Sheol) are pictured as a shadowy abode of spirit beings, who seemingly fade gradually into oblivion, whereas the New Testament contains quite a different picture of paradise and the heavenly abode, where God "shall wipe away all tears from their eyes." In contrast with the rewards of heaven, there are the punishments of Gehenna, "where the worm does not die, nor is the fire ever extinguished."

Any recognition of a progressive revelation in Scripture, and particularly of any significant difference between the Old Testament and the New Testament, must inevitably involve certain differences in presuppositions. This does not rule out divine inspiration, but it does mean that the revelation took place within the context of real events and different patterns of behavior and thought.

3. *Supernatural beings.* So much is a personal sovereign God a basic presupposition of the Bible, that at no place is God described or defined, or God's existence proved. God is simply taken for granted as the most basic presupposition about the supernatural world. But the existence of other supernatural beings, such as angels, demons, and the devil, also rests on basic presuppositions. Furthermore, supernatural beings are regarded as having power to bless and to curse, to reward faithfulness and to punish neglect. They communicate with persons by apparitions, dreams, visions, and through the drawing of lots, and human beings may communicate with the

supernatural by means of prayer and, in the context of the Old Testament, through sacrifices and offerings. In addition, certain objects could be so impregnated with supernatural power that they could not be handled by persons not specially consecrated to do so, as in the case of the ark of the covenant.

To say that all of these events and objects represent basic cultural presuppositions is not to make any judgments as to their reality. They were simply taken for granted and their power was not questioned. Jesus speaks of the crippled woman whom he had healed on the sabbath as "this descendant of Abraham whom Satan has kept in bonds for eighteen years" (Luke 13:16).

4. *Interpersonal relations.* Presuppositions about interpersonal relations are often the most complex. The concept of group responsibility and hence corporate guilt may pose special problems of understanding; but such a presupposition is necessary, if one is to make any sense of many of the accounts of the Old Testament, such as the guilt of Achan at the conquest of Ai (Josh. 7:1-26). The acceptance of slavery as a legal institution, the dominance of husbands over wives (in matters of divorce and property rights), and the irretractable nature of paternal blessings (Gen. 27), all rest upon important presuppositions about interpersonal relations.

5. *Intellectual activity.* Presuppositions about the validity of certain types of intellectual activity may be particularly difficult for persons in another culture to understand or to appreciate. From the biblical viewpoint, for example, truth is not an abstract definition of reality or being but is essentially right thinking about moral behavior, and wisdom is not intellectual capacity to formulate philosophical questions and provide cogent systems but rather the ability to decide moral and human issues with justice. The symbols of light and darkness are not related in the Bible to knowledge and ignorance, but to deliverance from or slavery to evil. And "to know" the Lord, sin, or deliverance, is not to "know about" such objects or events, but to experience them.

But presuppositions about valid intellectual activity also involve the acceptability of certain procedures for ascertaining what is true. For example, the use of quotations in the Scriptures differs markedly from what present-day scholars would regard as acceptable canons of proof. The Gospel of Matthew (2:15), for example, cites "Out of Egypt have I called my son" (Hos. 11:1), even though in the original context the reference is clearly to the people of Israel and not to the Messiah. Similarly, the Gospel of Mark announces a citation from Isaiah, though the first part of the quotation actually comes from Malachi. In the Letter to the Hebrews (1:7), a citation from the Old Testament in which God makes the winds his angels and flames of fire his servants is quoted in an inverted form, "God makes his angels winds and his servants flames of fire."

Such procedures for quotation of Old Testament texts were quite in keeping with the contemporary presuppositions about the use of sacred texts.

Unless one understands the New Testament usage in this light, one can become seriously confused. When Paul makes a point of the Old Testament use of "seed" and not "seeds" as a reference to Christ (Gal. 3:16), one should not conclude that Paul was unaware of the fact that in reality "seed" in this context referred to "descendants" or "lineage." He was simply using canons of scriptural reference that were completely acceptable in his day, and was arguing with the Judaizers in a way that they would have accepted as fully valid. But such use of the Scriptures rests upon presuppositions about verbal proofs that are in general foreign to present-day assumptions about how authors should be cited.

These types of presuppositions, which are so basic to any adequate comprehension of the meaning of any communication, do not, however, exist in a vacuum, even though for the most part they are never verbalized. Being so fundamental to a people's whole outlook, they do not require specification; no one feels any obligation to state the obvious. But to state that the presuppositions are not verbalized does not mean that they are empty rationalizations. Quite the contrary, they are constantly manifested in the daily life of the people of any culture, both in the recurring cultural patterns of behavior and in the ways in which people understand and interpret events.

Patterns of Behavior

Patterns of behavior are those recurring events that are typical of any society, and it is through such actions that the basic presuppositions about life and values become most readily known. The casting of lots to determine innocence or guilt, the use of Urim and Thummim in deciding issues, the use of ashes from the altar in ordeals, and sexual abstinence before going into battle are indices of significant presuppositions about how supernatural guidance and help may be obtained. The emphasis upon names, the importance of verbal blessing and cursing, and the creation of the world through "speaking," all indicate an assumption about the power of words. The importance of levirate marriage, the virginity of the bride, and the use of a wife's maid to beget children (who are then reckoned as those of the wife), all point to certain presuppositions about interpersonal relations of marriage and sex that are quite foreign to modern society. Similarly, the symbolic values assigned to sheep and goats, touching the horns of the altar, and swearing by the "loins" (in reality, the genitals) likewise suggest quite a different set of assumptions about the value of certain objects and actions.

Even more important, however, than the recognition of such patterns of behavior as having underlying presuppositions distinctive of the so-called biblical culture is the fact that these different patterns and their respective assumptions form a consistent whole. This does not mean that they are consistent from the outsider's viewpoint, but within the structure of which they are a part they constitute a meaningful set of integrated relations.

Interpretation of Events

Not only do the sets of recurring patterns of behavior indicate quite clearly underlying presuppositions about reality and values, but the ways in which events are interpreted also signal important elements in the presuppositions. At one particularly crucial time the Israelites, having suffered severe defeat at the hands of the Philistines (1 Sam. 4–5), insisted on taking the Ark of the Covenant into battle, because they were confident that this would protect them from defeat. But despite the presence of the Ark, the Israelites were defeated. The Philistines, however, were soon stricken with bubonic plague, and they interpreted this epidemic as punishment from the God of Israel and accordingly sought to placate him by returning the Ark with several gold mice and replicas of bubonic tumors. The presuppositions about the "positive taboo" associated with objects such as the Ark are essential to the understanding of the actions of both the Israelites and the Philistines.

Similarly, in the story of Achan at Ai the magnitude of the guilt can be understood only in the light of the ancient practice of *herem*—that is, consecrating everything to destruction in honor of the deity. Any violation of such a procedure, at least in theory, was regarded as nothing short of sacrilege. Furthermore, Achan's sin implicated his entire family, in view of the prevailing concepts of corporate guilt; hence the stoning of Achan and all his household seemed a completely fitting punishment for such defilement.

In many instances, the interpretation of events involves no such serious issues, but the understanding of an event may depend very much on certain presuppositions. For example, in John 4:27 one reads that the disciples were "greatly surprised to find Jesus talking with a woman." Most persons today would be surprised if Jesus did not take advantage of the opportunity to speak to a woman so evidently in need. But it is only in the light of the Jewish tradition that insisted "no Rabbi would speak with a woman" that one can fully understand the surprise of the disciples.

This same story, however, may give rise to an entirely different interpretation in societies having quite a different set of presuppositions about behavior. For example, in some places a request for food or water from a woman under such circumstances (when there was evidently no one else around) is almost always interpreted as a request for sexual relations. It is quite impossible in a translation designed for the people of such a society to change the story of Jesus' conversation with the woman, but it is certainly essential that some marginal note be employed to explain correctly what was intended by Jesus' remark and how the subsequent surprise of the disciples is to be understood.

The cultural presuppositions, the behavioral patterns that reflect such presuppositions, and the interpretations that persons give to objects and events all constitute a unified whole. One simply cannot change any part without immediately running into problems with certain other aspects of the system. For example, some persons have insisted that the demoniac who claimed that his name was "Legion" was really suffering from an inferiority complex, and that the translation of this story should make this clear. But if the demoniac were to reply to Jesus that he had an inferiority complex rather than being possessed by a "Legion," his insight would have been rather anachronistic, to say the least, and such insight is not normal for persons who are so deranged. But an even more complicated problem results from the rest of the story. It may be one thing to free a man from an inferiority complex, but quite another thing to cast such a complex into a herd of swine.

Whether a modern translator believes in demons or not is not the issue. What is important is that the Gospel writers took them seriously, and it is the viewpoint of the Gospel writer and not one's own presuppositions which should be reflected in a translation.

One Bible translator attempted to produce a version of the New Testament designed for rural, uneducated people in the southern United States. In one of his earlier attempts Jesus is said to have been born in a shack, because there was no room in the motor court. But this type of "modernization" of the account immediately involves a cultural transposition, which produces a credibility gap for the rest of the story. Motor courts simply do not fit in a land where camels and donkeys were the chief means of transportation. The historical setting of events, the cultural presuppositions, and the interpretations of events are all woven into the same biblical fabric. If the translator cuts into it at one point, it unravels throughout. Consequently, if one does attempt to culturally transpose when rendering the biblical message, it is essential that one be consistent and go the whole way.

This is precisely what Clarence Jordan did in the Cotton Patch Version, in which Rome becomes Washington, Annas and Caiaphas are co-presidents of the Southern Baptist Convention, and Jesus is lynched rather than crucified. However, Jordan was unable to maintain a complete transposition, and as Paul sails to Rome in Acts 27–28 the story reverts to its original historical setting, rather than having Paul make a quick jet trip.

It is important to note that this culturally adapted version, although excellent in many ways, has not been adopted or appreciated by those who are socially, educationally, economically, and geographically closest to the cultural transpositions that have been introduced. Only those persons who for special reasons are sympathetic with Jordan's view of church and society have been able to appreciate the none-too-subtle irony of these cultural modernizations.

3
Translating Means Communicating

Having discussed the various factors that enter into the communication of a message within a single language (and primarily in terms of the biblical languages as the source languages), we must now analyze the applications of communication theory for the problems of translation—that is, the transferring of a source-language message into a receptor language. The model for this involves the same essential elements as for communication within a language: the source, the message, the receptors, the setting, and the interpretive frame of reference.

The Receptor-Source

Translators, who can be regarded as the immediate source of translations, always play a double role, inasmuch as they are both receptor and source, but they are basically secondary receptors (unless they happen to participate in an original communication—for example, in so-called simultaneous interpreting). Normally they should be persons who speak the receptor language as their mother tongue but who have a completely adequate comprehension of the source language. The source language and its cultural context, however, may have been learned through the medium of a world language, which may or may not be the translator's own.

More fundamental, however, than knowledge of a language and its cultural frame of interpretation are the attitudes that translators have toward such languages, because their emotional identification with one or another language is crucial. Translators, for example, who are more in love with Greek or Hebrew than with their own mother tongue are likely to prove very poor Bible translators. They will almost inevitably feel constrained to carry over into their own language some of the forms that they have learned to appreciate in the foreign tongue.

On the other hand, it is also possible for translators to become so enamored of a receptor language they have studied (especially when they have reduced such a language to writing and thus tend to regard it as "their own") that they may want to "purify" it of all foreign borrowings or may think that its exotic differences must all be preserved for posterity by being incorporated into the Scriptures. It is not easy for one to be in love with a language and at the same time be completely objective about its strengths and

20

weaknesses—and all languages have both. But translators need to be sufficiently informed in their study of literary potentialities of a receptor language in order to be objective.

The Message

Perhaps the most difficult task for any translator is to think of the message in terms of the receptor-language frame of interpretation based on the presuppositions and values of the culture. Having studied the message in the source language, a translator almost inevitably understands it in the light of this language-culture context. But this is precisely what the average receptor cannot do. Being unacquainted with the source language (otherwise there would be no need for a translation), the receptors must interpret the message in terms of the only frame of interpretation that they have—namely, their own receptor culture.

Because translators always recognize, at least to some extent, this problem of disparity between the source and receptor languages (and their corresponding sets of presuppositions and values), there is usually some effort made to correct what may seem to be crucial difficulties. One type of correction that leads to many errors is borrowing—that is, introducing into the receptor language those foreign terms that will presumably carry the content that they have in the source language. But they rarely do so. Words that are borrowed by the translators themselves (not those that have been borrowed at an earlier time and may have already been "naturalized," even to the point where many receptors are not aware of their borrowed status) do not come into the language clothed in their proper content. In fact such words may be said to enter a language entirely naked. They have to be given their semantic clothes from association with certain objects and events. Such a word may also be said to be a "zero" word; it is not nothing, but a significant absence of something. This means that it will inevitably be given some content, but not necessarily the content that it had in the language from which it has been derived.

Early Roman Catholic missionaries in Latin America hoped to communicate the proper meaning of God by introducing the Spanish term *Dios* among Indians who had worshipped the sun as the supreme deity. But though *Dios* was borrowed, it soon acquired only the meaning of the sun-god, who was then called *Tata Dios*, "Father God." In one of the languages of Africa Protestant missionaries insisted on borrowing the Greek *pneuma* (in the form of *nyuma*) for "spirit," even though the indigenous language contained numerous terms for spirit. Similarly, Roman Catholics borrowed *Espiritu* (from Latin *spiritus*) for the same local language. But both Protestant and Roman Catholic catechists had to explain these terms by indigenous expressions, and they happened to employ precisely the same forms in doing so. In the end nothing had really been gained, for the borrowed words simply came to be interpreted in the light of already existing beliefs. This does not mean that borrowed terms are never legitimate, but it does mean that filling them with content is not an easy task. In general, descriptive phrases are much better than borrowed foreign terms.

Media and Channels

Because Christian faith, especially in its Protestant forms, has been traditionally expressed so preeminently in verbal forms, it is sometimes difficult for Christians to realize that the communication of religion in other societies may employ quite different media. In many religions very little is said about one's beliefs. In fact there may be no formalized statement about the tenets of such a faith. Individuals are not instructed in religion; they are simply expected to practice it by offering gifts to the ancestors, sacrificing to the gods of the forest, or pouring libations to the spirits of the animal world. They learn by performing its rituals, not by being catechized. In fact many Hindus refuse to engage in religious dialogue: they claim that it is contrary to the very nature of religion, for religion is something to be experienced rather than to be discussed. They contend that to experience is to know, and merely to talk about religious beliefs is to miss their true meaning.

It is precisely the emphasis upon the catechetical or verbal role of Christianity that makes it seem so much more like classroom instruction (like going to school) than like worship. In fact, when some Africans have been asked if they are Christians, they have explained their negative reply by adding, "But we have not learned to read." It is quite possible in some forms of Christianity to know a great deal about God without knowing God, and to be instructed in the faith without really believing. This does not mean that the verbalization of religious experience is unimportant, but it is basically secondary and derivative. Formulations of doctrines are only descriptions of reality; they are not the reality themselves.

The basic problem for Bible translating is that in so many cultures religion is not primarily an object of verbal discourse, but a series of ritual events by which human being's relation to supernatural powers and realities are "reenacted." In a sense this is precisely the strength of many pentecostal and charismatic movements, with their emphasis upon experience rather than upon intellectual comprehension.

The problems of channel are, however, equally as serious as those involving the communication media. At present great emphasis is placed upon the distribution of the Bible to those outside the Christian community. This is both important and strategic, but it involves a number of problems that are directly related to the form of the message itself, because the Bible was not produced primarily as a message for those outside the community of faith. It was essentially a message for those who had already accepted the faith.

The books of the Old Testament were written primarily as a record of God's dealing with persons within the covenant relation. These books gained a considerable audience in the ancient pagan world because they contained such a relatively high set of moral and ethical values and because they differed so conspicuously from the myths about the nature gods of the Greeks and Romans. But the Old Testament was never designed to serve as a vehicle of evangelism or proselytism. As to the New Testament, the Epistles in particular were directed to the peculiar problems of the believing communities, and even the Gospels were written first and foremost for the establishment of the faith among believers. Secondarily, these documents were evidently intended to serve the important purpose of assisting the witness of those who communicated their faith to others, by providing in written form a substitute for the personal witness of those who had been with Jesus but who were dying off in increasing numbers by the time the Gospels were composed.

Though the Scriptures were designed to accompany the witness of the believing community, they were not prepared as "tracts for popular distribution." In fact, in the ancient world the cost of books was relatively so high that widespread distribution of the biblical message through handwritten scrolls was quite impossible. Though literacy was almost universal in the ancient world, its use was far more commercial than recreational, and few persons were wealthy enough to have libraries.

At the present time, however, the churches and the Bible Societies have undertaken to distribute the Bible in relatively inexpensive editions to many persons who are entirely untouched personally by the church. The Bible is thus not simply a confirmatory document used by the church in its word-of-mouth witness, but is an "instrument of evangelism"—in fact, it has been called "the cutting edge of evangelism." This means, however, that the Scriptures are being used as a channel quite different from the original one.

Because some persons wish the Bible to go where the missionary cannot go, and some even intend for the New Testament alone to produce a "New Testament church," it is not strange that new demands are being placed upon the Bible and the translator. Some persons, for example, would like to have the translator "fill out the text," adding all the background information that may be useful to present-day readers, so that they may understand everything that the original reader did. This would mean producing a combination of commentary and translation, much like the ancient Targums written for the Jewish people when many among them could no longer readily understand Hebrew. Others would go even further and insist that the Bible itself be rewritten, to contain the same truths but in entirely new cultural clothing. This would mean both reinterpreting the contents and re-editing the style to fit modern readers.

Most persons, however, strongly reject the idea that the Bible should be rewritten, because they respect too much the historical setting of God's revelation and have too high a regard for the integrity of the documents themselves. They insist, however, that certain background information must be given in marginal helps, so that the present-day reader can understand the distinctive features of the biblical account. They also realize that certain adjustments must be made within the text itself, but obviously there must be limits to such adjustments. Otherwise the translation ceases to be really a translation and becomes a kind of running commentary.

There is, however, no general agreement as to what can and should be done to make the Scriptures more meaningful to persons of today. The fundamental reasons for the need to do something different from what has been the traditional practice are due in large measure to the distinctively different way in which the Scriptures are now being used as a channel of communication. The solution to these problems is the essential concern of the final chapters of this book.

The Receptors

In any original communication a competent source quite naturally attempts to anticipate the ways in which receptors are likely to respond to or interpret the message. This means that the source employs what might be called "anticipatory feedback"—that is, sensing in advance how an audience is likely to react to what is said. As a result, the writer chooses words and employs discourse forms that will be effective in communicating the message.

Anticipatory feedback is actually the mechanism behind the development of the rhetorical style known technically as "diatribe," a type of philosophical argumentation that takes up one by one the possible arguments of one's opponents and attempts to answer them. Such rhetorical devices are quite common in the Pauline Epistles, especially the Epistle to the Romans where the opposition arguments are frequently identified as such and in some cases imaginary opponents are even addressed by the use of the second person plural (Rom. 2:1, 17; 3:1; 6:1; 7:1; 9:19).

Though authors should be expected to employ some measure of anticipatory feedback with respect to their original set of receptors, one cannot expect them to anticipate the ways in which all persons at all times and under all circumstances will react to what they say. In a sense it is translators who must employ anticipatory feedback as they direct the message to an audience different from the first. Translators, however, do not have the privileges of the original author—namely, to edit, restructure, and revise the original work on the basis of possible criticism. Translators must reflect the manner in which the original author anticipated the problems of comprehension on the part of the original audience, but translators can assist their own audience by producing a text that does not mislead the reader. Therefore, in the wording of the translation and in the supplementary information it contains, the text should be a clear and accurate representation of the message as communicated by the original author, so that the receptors of the translated message will not misunderstand how the original receptors must have understood the message.

How the receptors of a translation interpret the form and content of a message depends in considerable measure upon the extent to which they understand the original language-culture setting. If they understand the presuppositions and values and comprehend the meaning of the various behavioral patterns, they will have little or no difficulty in deciding what the original message must have meant to the first receptors. If, however, they lack this information and if they have no ready access to such data, it is inevitable that they will understand the message of the translation only in terms of their own frame of interpretation, in which their own cultural presuppositions and values play a dominant role. For example, if receptors have no knowledge of the practice in ancient times of a man "marrying his sister" (probably a reference to a practice similar to the Hurrite tradition of adopting a wife as a sister, as a means of facilitating transfer of property rights), they can only interpret Abraham's relation to Sarah as being incestuous, and they may very well conclude that Sarah's sterility was a fitting divine punishment.

More crucial to an interpretation of the biblical message, however, are the "holy wars," in which not only men, but women, children, and even cattle are slaughtered. Such events are not only abhorrent to the so-called civilized world (though the bombing of civilian populations is a modern parallel), but they are equally inexplicable to many so-called primitive peoples, who simply cannot understand why women and children were not permitted to live, to be adopted into the tribal group, and thus to increase the strength and well-being of the community. The destruction of cattle is thought to be even more senseless.

Without some understanding of the presuppositions about the hallowed character of the Sabbath, most readers completely miss the point of the Pharisees' objection to what Jesus' disciples did on the Sabbath day as they went through a wheat field and plucked, threshed, and ate the grain. Readers can see the reprehensible nature of "stealing the grain," but they cannot understand how anyone could or should object to threshing and eating it.

For societies where spitting is used to convey a blessing (e.g., the Shilluks in the Sudan), the fact that Jesus spat upon the tongue of a man as part of the process of healing his dumbness is understandable; but to many others this use of spittle seems not only strange but repulsive.

Sensitive translators will recognize that many accounts in the Scriptures produce misunderstanding. But what are they to do? They cannot change the nature of the account and still be faithful to the text that they are translating, for they are translators; they are not the original writer. Some translators have felt that they should introduce into the text all the information that might be useful in providing background for a full understanding of a passage, but to do this would be to violate the authenticity of the original communication. No such explanation was necessary in the original communication, because the receptors shared with the source the same background data and presuppositions. To translate as though the original receptors did not understand how to comprehend the message would introduce an anachronistic element that could be fatal to a proper appreciation of the historical integrity of the message. But to do nothing about such background information can be equally misleading.

Despite the lack of background information, however, many readers of the

Bible seem not to be unduly disturbed by what they do not understand or by what they judge to be contradictory or inconsistent. Many have been taught that the Bible cannot contain any errors, and therefore they conclude that any problems of comprehension must be their own fault and not that of the text. In fact, however, most persons simply put their confidence in someone whom they regard as a competent guide in such matters, and they conclude that since someone else has faced the problems and has continued to believe, they can and should do likewise. If the church possesses a particularly strong "sense of community" (and especially if it has important social, economic, and legal force), persons will remain at least nominal or statistical members of the community, despite almost total lack of active faith. In a sense they possess a kind of schizophrenic religious experience, with two different sets of ideas that have not been resolved, and often two different sets of behavior reflecting these differences.

A more satisfactory approach to the differences and conflicts between presuppositions in the biblical and receptor cultures consists in understanding enough of the background of biblical life and times to appreciate the manner in which the divine revelation has come in the midst of these cultural assumptions, and even despite them. It is only then that one begins to comprehend certain of the unique features of the biblical revelation: God's initiative in seeking humankind, a concept of history that looks forward to the rule of justice, the transformation of human beings through love, and the unparalleled personality and ministry of Jesus.

But in the same manner as God was revealed in the person of the Son, who had "emptied himself" of certain divine prerogatives, so the revelation of God in the biblical record can be understood only within the limitations imposed by the presuppositions and cultural patterns of the language-culture setting. These insights are not something that the translator can translate into the text of the Scriptures; they must come as the result of the teaching of the "believing community." The translator can only provide a limited amount of adjustment and supplementary information. A translation is not a substitute for a commentary, nor is a text of Scripture equivalent to a sermon.

Diverse Sets of Presuppositions

In previous sections the presuppositions and values of a culture have been spoken of as though they constituted a single consistent whole. This is, however, by no means the case. Within the Bible itself there are quite different presuppositions. The henotheism (that is, one God superior to all others) of certain parts of the Old Testament gives place to monotheism, which denies the very existence of other gods. The sacrificial system of the Old Testament is completely rejected in the New Testament. The polygamy of the Old Testament is set aside in the New Testament. Jesus himself referred to certain aspects of the law as "you have heard it was said," and then proceeded to give the law a quite different interpretation and relevance. It was precisely the differences in presuppositions that gave rise to the first conflict within the church—namely, the manner in which Gentiles were to be admitted to the fellowship.

Not only does the Bible reflect different sets of presuppositions of ancient Palestinian life, it also contains references to certain Greco-Roman presuppositions of the ancient world. The Johannine writings clearly indicate the struggle of the early church against the beliefs of Gnosticism, which were based on a primordial dualism of spirit and matter and which sought to interpret the incarnation and the resurrection in dualistic terms, thus allowing for the death of Jesus and the resurrection of Christ.

If one is prepared to recognize differences of presuppositions in the Bible, it is even more necessary to realize that there are quite different sets of cultural assumptions in most present-day societies. Within the western world, for example, the "scientific viewpoint" is supposed to represent the thinking of "modern man," but this is far from being generally true. Perhaps most intellectuals possess a "scientific, secular view of the world," which might be characterized roughly as (1) an explanation of life on the basis of biological evolution, (2) a mechanistic interpretation of the universe, requiring no "supreme intelligence," (3) an interpretation of history based essentially on purely human forces operating within certain ecological limits, and (4) a set of ethical values that are derived from human nature and are essentially humanistic. Along with such views of the world go a rejection of supernatural beings, a repudiation of magic, and lack of interest in religious activities.

But for a majority of persons in the modern world, this scientific view of life is quite foreign. They may have rejected established religions, but they have certainly not given up clairvoyance, astrology, mediums, witches, and amulets (such as rabbits' feet, lucky pennies, and images). Some may even claim a "scientific view" in certain contexts of life, but they fear a curse from a good person and they seek healing from those claiming "miracle cures." In fact, many persons, despite their formal adherence to one or another system of thought, have strange mixtures of belief, and rarely if ever do they attempt to resolve the underlying contradictions: they believe what they want to believe. In a sense they are "spreading their risks," and they seem to be as content with second-hand doubts as with second-hand faith.

In view of the important differences of presuppositions that may exist within a single society, it is not surprising that there are vast differences between the biblical culture and other cultures in the world. One might assume that the differences would be particularly striking if one compared the culture of the Bible with that of some present-day society in Central Africa. In reality, however, they have much in common: polygamy, belief in miracles, the practice of blessing and cursing, slavery, systems for revenge, sacrifice, and communications through dreams and visions. The pastoral Navajos see much in the Bible that is parallel to their own way of life: tending sheep, casting out evil spirits, corporate responsibility, discerning the weather by the sky, foretelling events, and the expectation of the end of this world (after which great changes will be instituted).

In a sense the Bible is the most translatable religious book that has ever been written, for it comes from a particular time and place (the western end of the Fertile Crescent) through which passed more cultural patterns and out from which radiated more distinctive features and values than has been the case with any other place in the history of the world. If one were to make a comparison of the culture traits of the Bible with those of all the existing cultures of today (one would have to reckon with some two thousand significantly different groups of persons), one would find that in certain respects the Bible is surprisingly closer to many of them than to the technological culture of the western world. It is this "western" culture that is the aberrant one in the world. And it is precisely in the western world, and in the growing number of persons in other parts of the world who share its worldview, that the Scriptures have seemingly the least ready acceptance.

One of the important developments in Christianity that reflects this difference in cultural outlook is the rapidly growing number of "indigenous churches." It is estimated that in Africa alone, within the last twenty years more than fifteen million persons have become related to the "independent" or "separatist" churches, which for the most part find themselves at home with the Bible but alienated from the traditional institutions of western Christianity. Instinctively these persons feel an identity with the Bible, but they feel out of place in traditional western churches, which in so many ways no longer reflect "the life and faith of the Bible."

Though one cannot face fairly the problems of the translator without reckoning with the many and often striking differences between the culture of the Bible and that of other societies, it would be quite wrong to exaggerate the diversities, as some persons have done. As anthropologists have frequently pointed out, there is far more that unites different peoples in a common humanity than that which separates them into distinct groups. Such cultural universals as the recognition of reciprocity and equity in interpersonal relations, response to human kindness and love, the desire for meaning in life, the acknowledgment of human nature's inordinate capacity for evil and self-deception (or rationalization of sin), and its need for something greater and more important than itself—all these universals are constantly recurring themes in the Bible. These are the elements in the Scripture that have appealed to numberless persons through the centuries and across cultural frontiers.

What is important about recent interest in the Bible in the western world is the very fact that the Scriptures come from another age and from a distant culture. For a long while modern persons have been told that their problems are the direct result of their technologically based life characterized by urbanization and industrialization, but now many are discovering that persons portrayed in the Bible had precisely the same problems and needs as persons today—the proclivity to sin even when they want to do right, the feeling of guilt, a need for forgiveness, power to resist temptation, and the desire to love and to be loved. The fact that these universal needs are exemplified within the context of concrete historical events involving real life is what makes the Bible so much alive and appealing to persons in so many societies.

Historical Setting of the Bible

As compared with the basic documents or verbal traditions of other religions, the Bible is unique in its portrayal of actual events involving specific human beings. Whereas the religious documents of Hinduism concern primarily the exploits of the gods, the Bible is concerned essentially with the activity of God in human history. And in contrast with the religious treatises of Buddhism (which contain primarily philosophically derived ethical principles) and with the Koran (which focuses upon the exhortations and warnings of the prophet), the Bible is rooted in history and consists primarily in recounting how God has entered history to reveal the divine power, will, and person. Biblical faith is thus firmly rooted in events—in a God who acts.

Moreover, the God of the Bible is portrayed as acting in specific instances and not merely in generalized ways. Thus the specific historical context of the biblical account acquires very important theological implications, and Christians have almost instinctively reacted against any attempts to transpose the cultural and historical context of the biblical accounts. In reaction to one attempt to transpose the biblical message into an African setting, a chief remarked, "If that was what really happened, then why did not our grandfathers tell us about it?" Making the biblical account too contemporary can, in fact, destroy some of its very credibility.

From the standpoint of Judeo-Christian biblical theology, the entrance of God into history at specific times and places is both relevant and crucial. It is obvious, therefore, that the events recorded in the Bible cannot be altered. If, however, a certain event depends for its meaning upon a set of presuppositions that are conspicuously different from those of the receptor culture, what is the translator to do to prevent serious misunderstanding? In the first place, the translator cannot hope to make the message so clear that any reader can fully understand it without any reference whatsoever to the presuppositions that underlie the biblical account. That is to say, the translator cannot be expected to so transpose the message linguistically and culturally that it will fit completely within the interpretive frame of the receptor culture. To do this would mean to rob the message of its distinctive time-space setting. Furthermore, the translator's purpose is not to make the message sound as though the events took place in a nearby town only a few years ago. Rather, the objective should be to so translate (and with the translation to provide such background data) as to prevent receptors from misunderstanding what the original receptors understood when they first received the message.

Where the message seems merely unusual in terms of a particular receptor culture, the translator is not required to make adjustments or provide supplementary information; commentaries are designed to do this very thing. Where, however, a translation results in a text that would have a contrary meaning or would be misleading or would seem meaningless, then something must be done, either through some adaptation in the text or by means of cross-referencing or by some marginal note, whether on the same page or in a glossary. Just how this is to be done and under what circumstances will be dealt with in Chapter 7.

One can be sympathetic with translators who wish to produce a translation that is at the same time a running commentary. As already noted, this is what the early Jewish Targums were—a blend of translation and commentary. They arose out of what might be called an "evangelistic concern," because many Jews could not understand the Hebrew text and so needed something that would make the text fully meaningful. Accordingly, the Aramaic Targums were prepared; but it is important to note that they were strictly limited in their usefulness and the principle of the Targums was not adopted in Christianity.

The targumizing tendency, however, still exists among some Bible translators, especially among those who prepare texts for presumably "primitive peoples." Since such peoples are not used to books and are often regarded as incapable of appreciating or understanding the differences between the text and the marginal helps, the argument is that certain radical adjustments, major inclusions, and supplementation of the text, for example, are required.

As a temporary expedient, such a procedure may have its value in tentative and preliminary materials, but in general the very persons for whom such texts are prepared soon repudiate them, once they acquire more knowledge about the Scriptures and the form that they have in major languages. A combination of translation and commentary is often repudiated as just another instance of paternalism on the part of those who have failed to see that even presumably primitive persons are intellectually capable of making important distinctions between the biblical account and necessary supplementary information.

The Difference between Exegesis and Hermeneutics

Exegesis may be described as the process of reconstructing the communication event by determining its meaning (or meanings) for the participants in the communication. Hermeneutics, on the other hand, may be described as pointing out parallels between the biblical message and present-day events and determining the extent of relevance and the appropriate response for the believer. Both exegesis and hermeneutics are included within the larger category of interpretation.

It is the task of the biblical scholar to provide insight into the problems of exegesis, and it is primarily the task of the preacher to help persons understand the relevance of the biblical message for the quite different language-culture settings of today. Some persons have misconstrued the preacher's task as being merely that of an exegete, and it is not difficult to see how this could have arisen, in view of some of the almost incredibly difficult translations of the Bible that have been in use. In fact, in one instance members of a translation committee objected to producing a clear translation of a particular passage, though they readily agreed as to its meaning and how it could be effectively and accurately expressed in the receptor language. They objected to producing a perfectly clear translation, and gave as their reason, "What then would the ministers have to do?" Obviously, with at least some of the exegetical difficulties resolved, the preachers could begin to preach, rather than merely to exegete such difficult passages.

The practical results of differences in the hermeneutics of the Scriptures depend in considerable measure upon whether the biblical cultural practice can be literally imitated. For example, if persons can imitate certain cultural features—resting on the seventh day, requiring long hair for women, abstaining from "unclean foods," and prohibiting women from speaking in church—they often do so, on the basis that the forms prescribed in the Bible must be preserved as being supracultural, even though the presuppositions that gave these forms their original significance are not accepted in the receptor culture. When these forms are carried over as regulations for present-day living, there is usually some attempt to insist on the validity of the accompanying presuppositions.

Most persons, however, interpret the biblical cultural forms in quite a different manner. They make no attempt to duplicate the formal features, but they try to understand the relation between the biblical cultural forms and the corresponding presuppositions and try to understand the relations, together with their meanings.

For example, when some of the Tzeltal believers in southern Mexico read Paul's admonition to refrain from marrying in order that God could be served more faithfully, they reasoned that for themselves at least quite the opposite situation prevailed. They felt that young people did not really settle down to serve the Lord with their whole hearts until they did get married, and therefore what was important in Paul's teaching was not abstinence from marriage but serving the Lord with complete faithfulness. This implied for the Tzeltals quite a different form from the one advocated by Paul for the Corinthians.

Some Protestants have taken special pleasure in citing Jesus' admonition not to call any man "father." They have studiously avoided this form, while failing to see that "reverend" or "doctor" implies precisely the same kind of class and rank distinction within a community of faith. Hermeneutics does not focus primarily upon the cultural forms but upon their relations to the presuppositions that do or should underlie them.

Somewhat more complex problems of hermeneutics occur when the biblical forms of behavior cannot be imitated or should not be practiced at the present time. Nevertheless, some persons insist that all the accounts described in the Bible must be accepted as fully justifiable actions. Accordingly, the exploits of revenge that Samson carried out against his enemies are regarded as justified vengeance, rather than as the tragic consequence of living by brute force. And Jacob's cleverness in cheating his brother Esau is similarly interpreted by many as predestined divine guidance rather than as a fearful failure in justice that contributed to generations of enmity, hatred, and suffering. A proper hermeneutics of the Scriptures can be based only upon the relations between the events and the associated presuppositions, as seen in the light of the whole biblical account and not from the narrow perspective of some momentary advantage.

On the basis of this type of hermeneutics preachers proceed to note parallels in modern life, and they do not have far to look. They may see in the story of the Good Samaritan a parallel in a black traveling salesman taking care of a member of the Ku Klux Klan who has been badly injured in an auto wreck; or the parable of the Prodigal Son may suggest a father welcoming home a hippie son who brings back a drug habit and venereal disease. The preacher's task is to lead the congregation in finding relevant parallels in modern life, and in discovering how persons can meaningfully live out the Good News in worship of God and in service to others.

Some theologians have insisted that the preacher's task must stop short of making an application and that laypersons must discover the implications of the text for themselves. But if preachers are only exegetes, they have adopted a role quite different from that of the ancient prophets, for the latter did not hesitate to declare how persons should right wrongs. The expository ministry of Jesus, largely through the use of parables, left no doubt as to what his followers should do if they wanted to "inherit the kingdom."

The task of the preacher, however, is quite different from that of the exegete and likewise very different from that of the translator. Hermeneutics, if it is to be effective, must depend upon linguistic and cultural transposition; but exegesis must confine itself to the detailed analysis of the original communication event, so as to provide a historically accurate and meaningful basis for later exposition. The translator must likewise provide the closest natural equivalent of the source-language message, so that it too may be employed effectively by receptor-language expositors in their task of transposition.

4
The Form of the Message

In any message there are two important elements that carry meaning: form and content. Both of these are especially crucial for the translator because they both involve a number of features requiring certain adjustments or supplementation if the meaning of the text is to be satisfactorily communicated.

The formal elements involve all formal features, from the transliteration of proper names to the literary genre. The meaning of these formal features is both cognitive and emotive. For example, the logical sequences of thought in a discourse (without regard to content) are basically cognitive, but ways in which such thoughts may be arranged and related may produce favorable or unfavorable emotive reactions.

The basic features of form involve primarily the following categories: (1) transliteration, (2) morphological structures (the structure of words), (3) phrase structures (the combination of words into clauses and sentences), (4) rhetorical devices (e.g., direct and indirect discourse, rhetorical questions, personification, chiasm, irony, hyperbole), (5) measured lines (i.e., poetic structures), (6) figurative language, (7) discourse structure (i.e., the organization of content in narrative, descriptive, argument, and dialogue discourse), and (8) literary genre (e.g., apocalyptic, prophetic, legislative, epistolary).

Everyone will agree as to the importance of adjustments in the meanings of certain words and phrases, but some persons overlook almost completely the problems of adjustments in purely formal features, for they seem to carry little or no meaning and therefore would seem to be more or less mechanical elements in the translator's task of transferring a message from the source to the receptor language. It is quite true that some of the so-called lower levels of structure (sounds, word classes, and syntax) involve largely obligatory adjustments, though these are not without certain subtle differences of meaning; and the so-called higher levels of structure (e.g., rhetorical features, discourse structures, literary genres) involve much more optional elements. But it is precisely in the area of optional elements that a translator has some of the most difficult decisions to make. These aspects of language involve important values, for they are so intimately related to matters of style.

Even though these formal features of language seem to be much less important than the content of a message, they are nevertheless extremely significant and must be seriously considered before any really satisfactory analysis can be made of the translational difficulties involving content, which are considered in Chapter 5.

Transliteration

The transliteration of proper names poses a number of problems, largely because of the essentially arbitrary nature of the sound structures of different languages. Ideally, one should be able to take the form of a proper name as pronounced in the source language and adjust it to the closest natural phonological form in the receptor language. This would mean finding the closest corresponding sets of sounds and producing them in sequences that would not violate the normal sequences within the receptor language.

But rarely have proper names been systematically transliterated. Often the base has fluctuated between two or more source languages. For example, Bible translators have sometimes used Greek as a base and in other instances Hebrew for the same names. Other translators have interposed Latin, in which Greek and Hebrew names have already undergone certain changes, and many other translators have simply adopted the forms of biblical names as they occur in certain modern European languages, usually the former colonial language of the area or the missionary's own mother tongue.

In many cases the base for transliteration has not been the pronunciation of a name but the traditional spelling, and often a quite different set of rules has been adopted, depending upon the familiarity of a name. For example, names already in use, due to some early contact with Christian missions, are often taken over either in a radically modified form or perhaps even in the artificially correct spelling of the official language, whereas rare names are completely adjusted to the form of the receptor language. Names such as *Matthew, James, John,* and *Peter* are thus left unchanged, but names such as *Jehoshaphat, Nebuchadnezzar,* and *Abimelech* are radically altered.

In many cases, however, translators have only carried the process of adjustment to a halfway mark. They may have eliminated certain awkward consonant clusters by introducing vowels to break up a long series, or they may have changed some consonants so that they would more readily go together, but they have rarely changed the overall length of names nor have they adjusted the names to the regular patterns for sequence of vowels. In some languages there are patterns of vowel harmony that determine the kinds of vowels that can follow each other in succeeding syllables. Some attention to these "rules" for sequences must be given if the resulting transliterations are to sound at all natural or to seem to be pronounceable.

Furthermore, in some languages, it is quite uncommon for proper names to have more than three or four syllables. Accordingly, some of the excessively long names in Scripture are reduced in overall length, in accordance with regular patterns of reduction that such languages possess. Some persons, however, have contended that it is quite unnecessary and even unwise to make such adjustments in form, because foreign names should sound strange and, if necessary, even be hard to pronounce. On the other hand, most native speakers of a receptor language are frankly offended by the arbitrary and awkward character of many transliterations. They may not wish biblical persons to be addressed in an unbecomingly familiar manner—for example, Saint James should not be "Saint Jimmy" and the Apostle John should not become "Jack," nor should the patriarch Jacob be addressed as "Jake." But the overall effect of retaining difficult transliterations, and thus of impeding public reading of the Scriptures, is normally quite negative, and persons react to such forms as being unjustifiably foreign, difficult to pronounce, and hard to remember.

In some instances the objection to certain transliterations is based upon hostility to the people who speak the language used as a basis for the transliteration. For example, some Turkish-speaking persons have strong emotional reactions against transliterations based upon Greek. They would much prefer to have transliterations based upon almost any other language. But attempting to change well-established transliterations of names is exceptionally difficult and risky. Persons often become strongly attached to such forms and their emotional reactions against change are usually quite strong. For example, changing "Maria" to "Mary" may seem to some persons like utter sacrilege.

Normally, one need not be concerned with making transliterated proper names seem too familiar, for they always bear the imprint of their foreign origin. What is important is that they not become stumbling blocks to oral reading and cause embarrassment to those who may not have remembered just how these strange names are to be pronounced. In a recent revision of the Spanish Bible, well over two hundred names were changed, at least in some details, with the result that for the most part readers have been very pleased, for now they can read the Scriptures with less fear of mispronouncing such names.

Morphological Structures

The various classes of words, such as nouns, verbs, adjectives, and adverbs, often occur with a number of grammatical categories. For example, number (singular and plural), class (or gender), case (agent, goal, instrument, etc.), and honorifics are often associated with nouns and pronouns; affixes of tense (e.g., past, present, and future time), aspect (the kinds of action, e.g., continuous, repeated, beginning, ending, and completed), and mode are normally associated with verbs. Adjectives and adverbs often show degrees of intensity—for example, comparative *(finer than those),* superlative *(finest of these),* and absolutive *(the very finest).*

Where the forms of words are obligatory (i.e., required by a particular syntactic construction), the translator has no choice but to make the necessary adjustments. The aspectual system of Hebrew verbs must be adjusted to the so-called tense system of most modern Indo-European languages. Similarly, in going from Greek to a typical Bantu language, the three genders of Greek (masculine, feminine, and neuter) must be adapted to the dozen or more classes of most Bantu languages. But where the morphological structures are optional rather than obligatory, the translator's task becomes much more difficult, because it must be decided in each instance whether the introduction of particular forms really fits the context.

Some translators have tried to match consistently the structures of the source language, and in so doing they have produced some very cumbersome translations. The distinction between singular and plural is normally obligatory in Greek and English, but in some languages it is optional; in fact, a plural affix is often employed only at the beginning of a discourse, with each subsequent reference to the nouns given in a form without the plural affix. If, however, one follows the pattern of Greek or English and reproduces each of the plural forms, the result will be awkwardly "overloaded" with plurals.

In a sense this is similar to what Charles B. Williams did in his translation of the New Testament into English. In many respects his translation parallels Goodspeed's text except for the excessive and awkward emphasis upon the punctiliar and continuative aspects of the Greek verbal forms. What is quite natural in Greek becomes unnatural and overdone in English. Williams was simply not sensitive to the differences between obligatory and optional categories.

Phrase Structure

Phrase structure includes what has been traditionally regarded as the syntax of clauses and sentences, and for the translator this is one of the principal areas of adjustment. One particularly common adjustment involves the length of sentences. For example, Romans 1:1-7 needs to be broken up into shorter sentences in almost all languages, because this type of complex epistolary formula is exceedingly rare. The need to translate event nouns by verbs may also require syntactic recasting of sentences, and the shift from passive to active inevitably involves rather radical changes in the positions of the grammatical "satellites" related to the verb nuclei.

The order of dependent clauses may also be an important factor in restructuring, because in some languages dependent clauses must come first, and in other languages they tend to follow the principal clause. In many languages they may occur on either side of the principal clause, often with very subtle differences in meaning.

Problems of attribution may constitute major difficulties in some languages. For example, in Acts 27:23, a literal translation of "there stood by me an angel of God whose I am and whom I serve" could mean in some languages that Paul belonged to an angel and served him, because in such languages such phrases are always attached to head words such as *angel,* and not to subordinate terms such as *God.* When attributives require recasting into verb expressions, they may likewise result in considerable alteration of the syntactic form, though not of the meaning. For example, "false prophets" may be rendered in some languages as "those who say they are prophets of God, but are not" or "those who proclaim falsehoods in the name of God," and "false Christs" may be "those who pretend they are Christ."

The treatment of coordinate and subordinate relations may be particularly complex. For example, in Romans 1:5, "grace and apostleship" is in Greek syntactically coordinate, but it is semantically subordinate and has accordingly been translated often as "the privilege of being an apostle" or "a commission as an apostle," while a later phrase "obedience of faith," though subordinate in syntactic structure, is semantically coordinate and hence has been rendered as "faith and obedience" or "to believe and obey."

In discussions of such problems, many translators insist that certain syntactic constructions "can be said" in the receptor language. This may very well be true, but it is important to know just how natural such expressions are and how frequently they are likely to occur in a particular kind of discourse. If some particular syntactic construction (e.g., a passive verb phrase) occurs in a translation of the Bible with a frequency 15 percent greater than what it would normally have in a comparable receptor-language text, the translator should make serious efforts to restructure some of the sentences. In general, more than 5 percent deviation is regarded as suspect, but because it is extremely difficult to match discourse types satisfactorily, a 15 percent deviation seems a much more reasonable figure with which to be concerned.

Rhetorical Devices

A great many different features of language structure and style could be included under rhetorical devices—for example, parallelism, chiasm, irony, overstatement, understatement, figurative language, embedded direct discourse, personification, rhetorical questions, parenthetical statements, exclamations. A brief discussion of a few of these devices should, however, be sufficient to highlight some of the basic problems.

Shifts between direct and indirect discourse are perhaps the most frequent changes in rhetorical features. Some languages require direct discourse throughout, so that a sentence such as "He charged them that they should tell no man" (Mark 9:9) must be rendered as "He charged them, 'You must not tell anyone.'" Some languages, however, go one step further, in that all implied discourse must be made explicitly direct. For example, "They praised God" must be altered to make it direct discourse, "They said, 'God is great.'" There are other languages in which indirect discourse is greatly preferred, and this means that one must change a number of direct quotes into indirect ones.

Most languages employ both direct and indirect discourse, and this can be especially helpful in dealing with some of the highly involved series of direct quotations that occur in some of the writings of the prophets, where as many as five different sets of inclusions may be found. By judiciously alternating between direct and indirect discourse, one can often make the relations much clearer than by attempting to translate literally in accordance with the Hebrew structure, which in general employs direct quotations.

Epistolary formulas are rhetorical devices that must often be altered so that the reader will know precisely who is writing to whom. Far more difficult, however, are the adjustments required in rhetorical questions. Some languages employ very few rhetorical questions, or when they do, they require that some answer be immediately given.

The rhetorical questions in Romans 8:31–35 are particularly dramatic, but rendered literally into some languages they are quite misleading. For example, in verse 34 the question "Can anyone, then, condemn them?" is followed immediately by a sentence that begins, "Christ Jesus is the one. . . ." Several more words must be read before realizing that it cannot be Jesus Christ who condemns. This would be even more misleading in a language that normally requires all answers to rhetorical questions to follow them immediately. In the first chapter of Hebrews the rhetorical questions are so complex and involved (because they include direct quotations, which are not in themselves questions), that a number of translations employ statements to render these questions.

One epistolary usage, "we" for "I," can be misleading in some languages, and hence must normally be altered, if the translator can be certain that the reference is to the first person singular. That certainly seems to be the case, for example, in Romans 1:5 "God has given me the privilege of being an apostle."

Double negatives, as means of emphasis, are quite common in Greek, but must be changed in translating into English. If a receptor language resembles Greek in this particular feature, the double negative may be effectively retained in some instances. Some positive-negative expressions, however, may be more effectively rendered in another form. For example, "not many days later" may be more naturally rendered as "a few days later," and "not a few" may be better expressed as "many."

Personification of inanimate objects or of events may constitute some difficulties in some languages; for example, "Lift up your heads, you gates" (Ps. 24:7), "Praise him, sun and moon" (Ps. 148:3), and "Death, where is your sting?" (1 Cor. 15:55). But most languages appear to employ at least certain types of personification. In fact, in many languages personification is much more common than in the biblical texts.

The translator's solution to problems involving rhetorical devices is not merely to make the formal adjustments required by a receptor language, so that the resulting forms may not be misleading or unduly perplexing. These rhetorical features carry certain impact, by virtue of the fact that they are not the ordinary ways of saying things, and they therefore contribute considerably to the style and value of the discourse. One cannot afford to level them down to trivial mundane expressions. If the rhetorical patterns of a receptor language result in losses in dramatic effect at one point, one should attempt to compensate at other points or in other ways, so as to reproduce something of the same level of impact and effectiveness that characterizes the original text.

Poetry

Translating poetry satisfactorily is perhaps the most difficult task that any translator has. So distinctive is poetry that it is often classified as one of the two distinctive discourse types, the other being prose. In reality, however, poetry is not quite that distinctive: almost any and all types of discourse (teaching, history, predictions, personal accounts, and attitudes) can be put into a poetic form, as didactic, epic, prophetic, or lyric poetry.

What is distinctive about poetry is not the basic discourse structure but the character of its lines, as measured by word stresses, phrase stresses, length of vowels, number of poetic feet, number of syllables and words, and formal parallelism. The means of measuring such lines differ greatly from one language to another, but there is always some basic system of length, usually involving patterned parallelism. The feature of rhyme, so common in west European languages, is relatively uncommon if one considers all types of languages and poetic structures.

Though the feature of measured lines is the most conspicuous element of poetry, it is by no means the only distinctive feature. Poetry ordinarily employs many more figurative expressions than does prose, and a poem as a whole may have one or more figurative levels of meaning. Poetry also tends to employ novel expressions, is relatively compact (i.e., communicates considerably more per phrase than does prose), is quite complex in syntactic structure, but usually has shorter sentences and clauses than corresponding prose discourse. No one of these features or combination of features is diagnostic for defining poetry in contrast with prose but, taken together in various combinations and in varying degrees, they do serve to describe poetic forms.

What is important for the translator, however, is that what may be regarded as quite good poetry in one language does not necessarily turn out to be good poetry in another. The denunciations of the enemies of Israel by the Old Testament prophets in poetic form are highly effective in Hebrew, but when translated into English or some other west European language, they are often lacking in true poetic quality. For one thing, present-day manifestos, ultimatums, and denunciations are not written in poetic form, and though in Hebrew the poetic structure was valuable in making the words of the prophets seem more fitting for divine messages, it is not possible to carry across that same quality in most other languages.

Most Bible translators have recognized the fact that poetic forms and values differ widely in various languages, but some still attempt to reflect the original structures by printing an essentially prose text as though it were poetry through the use of some type of poetic indentation of the lines. But merely printing prose as poetry does not make it poetry. In fact, when translated materials do not possess the essential features of poetry in receptor languages, they should not be printed as poetry; and if they are printed as poetry, then the system of the receptor language should be employed.

Failure to do this is especially conspicuous in the New English Bible, which uses a system of triple indentation that reflects only the accentual system of the Hebrew lines. There is no relation between this Hebrew poetic stress system and the normal kind of indentation employed in English poetry, which depends upon parallelism and subordination of thought. This attempt to impose a Hebrew accent system upon an English indentation system is both unnatural and bizarre.

One of the important features of Hebrew poetry is the parallelism of lines, with a number of variations that involve crossing of corresponding features (called chiasmus), positive and negative parallelism, correspondence of strophes, and so forth. The most troublesome structures for the translator are the completely parallel lines, in which two lines say essentially the same thing, but merely use different words. If a receptor language does not normally employ such thought structures, the resulting forms may be completely misleading. In the first place, the reader may think that the original author was being stupidly repetitious. But if the expressions do not appear to be completely redundant, the reader may conclude that the author is really trying to say something different, rather than emphasizing the first line by providing a completely parallel expression in the following.

In a number of instances, translators have tried to resolve such problems of complete parallelism by reducing the two lines to one, and in order to compensate for the loss of emphasis carried by the two lines in Hebrew, they have introduced emphatic elements to reflect something of the original thrust. Ronald Knox purposely set out to eliminate as much parallelism as possible in his translation of Hebrew poetry because he felt that such parallelism does not fit modern English style. Many persons will argue as to whether the elimination of the parallelism is justified, but all will agree that Knox was remarkably successful in doing so, while not distorting seriously the emphasis of the source text.

Because of the highly specialized features of poetry in any source language, it is often impossible to carry across into a receptor language even some of the most distinctive elements. Nevertheless, one must make every effort to try to compensate insofar as possible. This will almost inevitably mean employing a much higher percentage of figurative expressions than would be normal for nonpoetry in the receptor language. It may also mean employing in poetry a number of figures of speech that may be quite novel and new to the receptor language. This will inevitably tend to load the communication channel rather heavily, but such loading is to be expected in poetry where compactness is one of the important features.

What is particularly important for the translator is to determine the "meaning" of the poetic form in the receptor culture. Does it mean, as it does to most persons in the English-speaking world (though not necessarily to some subcultures, e.g., youth), that the contents are somewhat unreal and the message is not especially urgent? Does the artificiality of form suggest to readers that the content is likewise artificial? Is poetry appreciated for lyric utterances, but frowned upon for didactic or epic purposes? Answers to such questions as these are essential in helping the translator determine what types of passages in the Scriptures should be rendered as poetry and printed as such, and which discourses should be transformed into a correspondingly effective prose style.

Figurative Language

Under figurative language can be classified all figurative meanings of individual words and idioms—that is, combinations of words whose meanings cannot be deduced from the meanings of the individual parts. Such expressions are often spoken of as "semantically exocentric," inasmuch as the meaning of the whole is different from the sum total of the parts. Because figurative language is very closely related to the cultural specialities of any language community, such expressions can only rarely be translated literally. At this point we are not concerned with the particular manner in which figurative expressions differ from one language to another. What is important is that the use of figurative language is universal, and in varying degrees figurative expressions are used to express many types of experience, especially psychological attitudes and reactions.

Because figurative language is proportionately much less frequent than nonfigurative, it carries more impact. And because it is so highly specialized in meaning and so closely tied to distinctive cultural features and attitudes, its use heightens the emotive value of a communication by making it seem far more relevant and personal. But inasmuch as many idioms of a source language cannot be translated into a receptor language, this means that introducing nonfigurative substitutes inevitably involves some loss of impact. This is especially true of poetic passages, in which figurative language is such an important element.

The sensitive translator, aware of the loss of impact because so many idioms and figurative meanings cannot be taken over into the receptor language, must make some attempt to compensate for this loss by the cautious use of idioms that may be employed to translate nonidioms in the source-language text. For example, by rendering "peace" as "to recline in the heart," by translating "love" as "to hide another in one's heart," and by reproducing the meaning of "trust" as "to lean one's full weight upon," there is some possibility of compensating, at least in some measure, for certain losses.

The problem of loss of impact when translating idioms by nonidioms is interestingly reflected in the reactions of many to the translation of figurative language in the Bible. When they are told about the figurative expressions that other languages employ to translate what is expressed in nonfigurative language in English, they are normally surprised and pleased to see that the Bible can be so meaningful. When they learn, however, that some idioms of the Scriptures are also lost in the process of translating (e.g., "hunger and thirst for righteousness" may become "desire righteousness very much," and "inherit the earth" is rendered as "receive what God has promised," while "to gird up the loins of your mind" must often be rendered as "get ready in your thinking"), they feel that the Scriptures are being robbed of some of their meaning. In reality, there is no loss of referential meaning but there is a loss of impact, and this loss should be kept to a minimum.

This problem of corresponding levels of impact is, however, a quite different problem from the complications of translating the semantic content of figurative language. This set of difficulties is the concern of the next chapter.

Discourse Structure

There are four basically different types of discourse structure: narrative, description, argument, and dialogue. Narrative discourse consists in a series of temporarily related events and participants, descriptive discourse consists primarily in a series of spatially related characteristics of objects or events, argument consists in a series of logically related events, states, or circumstances, and dialogue consists essentially in a series of questions and answers or of statements and negations in which the related forms are highly conditioned by one another. In actual texts, there is usually a mixture of discourse types. What may begin as a narrative, often contains description; in argument there may be embedded narratives as well as dialogue. Dialogue (in this technical sense) must be distinguished from "conversation," which is much more likely to be structured as narrative, description, or argument.

Narrative discourse normally begins with some kind of time-space setting (i.e., when and where the event or events took place) and an introduction of at least some of the participants. The sequence of events then normally follows in temporal order, but there may be "flashbacks" in which the narrator wishes to fill in readers with prior information, or "flashforwards" in which the author informs the readers of something that happens or is likely to happen later in the story. Though there is usually a relatively strict correspondence between linguistic and temporal orders (i.e., events are normally described in chronological order), the use of flashbacks is by no means rare. In fact, they seem to be practically universal in effective storytelling. They should not be regarded as merely a technique by which the source is able to fill in information that may have been forgotten. On the contrary, flashbacks permit the storyteller to begin at a very crucial point; after having gained the attention of the hearers, the storyteller can then better afford to provide some of the necessary background information. Narrative discourse usually ends with some kind of summary statement or resolution of the plot, which explains the point of the story.

Descriptive discourse usually begins from one point and then proceeds systematically to detail the various characteristics of some object or event. The description of a person's appearance, for example, normally does not jump from hair color to size of feet and then to the breadth of the shoulders, but will often start with the head and then proceed spatially to other parts of the body. Another type of descriptive orientation may involve a series of characteristics organized in terms of a particular semantic domain. For example, a building may be described first on the basis of the type of construction, then on the basis of its floor plan, followed by its system of decor, and so forth.

Argument discourse may proceed along the lines of any type of logical relations—for example, cause-effect, reason-result, purpose-result, or generic-specific. One may state a general proposition and then provide all the reasons why such a statement is true, for instance.

What is important about discourse structures is the fact that the structures themselves carry meaning, particularly in terms of focus and emphasis, and only rarely can one alter discourse structures without changing substantially the intent of the author. For example, some persons have suggested that the story of the Prodigal Son would be much more effective if one began the account with the young man taking care of the pigs, as a last resort to keep body and soul together. The earlier events could then be introduced as flashbacks, and one could then describe his return and reception by his father. From the standpoint of making the story more "lively," this might be justified but it would seriously violate the discourse structure employed by Luke.

In fact, the prodigal son is not the central character of this story, as can be seen by comparing the three different stories in the fifteenth chapter of the Gospel of Luke. The central figures are the woman who lost the coin, the shepherd who lost one of his sheep, and the father who lost one of his sons. It is the rejoicing of the woman, the rejoicing of the shepherd, and the rejoicing of the father that constitute the salient theme of these stories, and the central character needs to be introduced at the very beginning of each of them. The story of the Prodigal Son is, in reality, a story about the love of God, not about the exploits of a wayward son.

In Mark 6:16-18 there is a particularly difficult record of events involving two major and some minor flashbacks. Some persons would prefer to restructure the story so that it would be entirely in temporal order. But if that is done, it is extremely difficult to highlight the concern of Herod, who heard about the preaching and healing ministry of Jesus and concluded that this must be John, whom he had beheaded. It is only in the light of the anxiety felt by Herod that the story about John the Baptist becomes relevant.

In many languages one cannot introduce flashbacks merely by using a pluperfect tense, as in English. It may be necessary, for example, to say, "Herod said this because some months before he sent men to seize John. . . ." The second major flashback may be introduced by "Herod put John in prison because previously John said that Herod should not have married Herodias, who was before that the wife of Herod's brother Philip. . . ."

What is important in this passage in the Gospel of Mark is not the sequence of events as such, but the relations between reason and result. For Mark, the significance in this story is the "why" of what took place, not primarily the events themselves. In some languages it may actually be necessary to reorder the passage so that the linguistic order parallels the historical order; but if this is done, the focal elements of the account must be clearly marked and the reasons for the actions must be explicitly stated in order to compensate for what is lost by the linguistic reordering.

In trying to translate a sequence of events in a systematic and faithful manner, one may find inferences of relations in the receptor language that may not exist in the source document. For example, in a translation of Mark 15:37–39, the relation between the loud cry uttered by Jesus, the tearing of the curtain in the temple, and the statement of the centurion may be misunderstood. Some persons may imagine that the centurion himself saw the temple curtain being torn and that this was the reason why he exclaimed that Jesus must be "the Son of God." The lack of such a connection may be signaled in some languages by an adversative particle at the beginning of verse 39; one might even begin a new paragraph at verse 39 as a means of signaling the break.

There are clearly a number of passages in the Scriptures in which a translator might very well want to introduce stylistic improvement. For example, Paul employs a number of anacoloutha, sentences that begin in one way but end with a different structure. Some translators would like to smooth out such ungrammatical expressions by filling in some appropriate expressions. However, Paul's intensely "full and overflowing style," signaled in part by these ungrammatical sequences, reflects accurately the spontaneous and involved movement of his thought. The syntactic breaks in the structure help to show something of the intensity of feeling that must have moved him when he dictated his letters.

The translator's task is not that of an editor. Translators are not to improve on the original but to carefully reflect it. This means, for example, that they should not try to clear up all the obscure connections between the thoughts expressed in the First Epistle of John, for the writer himself does not show the relations. In such matters the translator should not try to be a rewrite artist.

It is normally not too difficult to make adjustments in the order of clauses within a sentence, because one can usually compensate readily for possible shifts in emphasis or focus, but it is extremely difficult to tamper with the "sequence of thought" in a long discourse without introducing features of meaning that may be quite foreign to the intent of the source. In narrative discourse, one can legitimately make certain minor modifications in the order of elements within the setting and can justifiably shift somewhat the order of items within any one episode (i.e., a closely related set of events within a single time-space setting), but it is risky to undertake changes that go much beyond these boundaries.

Similarly, in the case of argument discourse, one might conceivably improve on some texts by shifting the order in which the specific concepts are related to the more generic statements, but this generally results in some distortion of the original intent. For example, some translators would like to begin John 1 by introducing "Jesus Christ, who was called the Word of God." No doubt such a text would be easier for some persons to understand, but it seriously distorts the structure of the first eighteen verses, which are carefully designed to lead up to the climax of the incarnation.

Some translators have also thought that it would be better to incorporate most of Genesis 2 within Genesis 1, so that a seemingly more consistent account of creation could result. Such an attempt no doubt stems from worthy motives, but it distorts the historical background of the documents and also confuses accounts that reflect very different theological orientations.

Not only in secular tradition, but especially in the history of the church's attitude toward the Scriptures, there has always been a very high regard for the integrity of the source documents. In considerable measure this reflects a deep sense of responsibility toward the original author. The translator's task has always been defined in terms of an accurate representation of what the original author intended to say, and not what the translator might prefer that author to have said.

It is true that if we knew more about the respective patterns of discourse structures in the source and receptor languages, we would be in a much better position to make more extensive alterations in form while still preserving the same focal and connotative values. But in view of the relatively restricted corpus of Old and New Testament texts and the prevailing limitations of our knowledge of discourse theory and its particular application to various receptor languages, there are far more chances of error than of valid solutions in radical alterations of the forms of discourse. Furthermore, in comparison with the rather obligatory structures of sounds, words, and syntax, discourse involves many more structural options. And even though the values of the corresponding discourse structures may not be identical, they are for the most part roughly equivalent.

Literary Genre

In all languages there are a number of different kinds of literary forms. Some of the most common include letters, biography, novels, essays, poetry, and narrations (or accounts) of events. In the Bible some of the most distinctive literary genres are found in apocalyptic writings (e.g., the Book of Revelation and major parts of Daniel and Ezekiel), prophetic utterances, legislative regulations, and collections of proverbs.

In a sense the Gospels represent a very special literary genre. They are not primarily biographical, though they do contain a great deal that is biographical in nature. They are essentially apologia documents, meant to convince readers of the truth of the revelation of God in Christ, and therefore they do not follow a strict biographical order of development, nor do they attempt to provide the kind of description and background information that one would expect of biographical treatments. The entire focus is upon the unique significance of Jesus Christ as the revelation of God, and for this purpose some of the more familiar features of human biography—for example, descriptions of personal appearance—are not relevant.

Inasmuch as the values of certain types of literary genres differ from language to language, it is not strange that some persons have thought that certain literary forms of Scripture are rather out of date and could be improved upon. One person, for example, has urged that the Pauline Epistles be completely redrafted as essays, and that in the case of the Epistle to the Romans, the structure be made to conform to a "legal essay."

For example, Romans 1:4 has been restructured as follows: "This man Jesus clearly identified himself as God's Son, our Superior and Administrator, in his display of divine spiritual supremacy by voluntarily enduring death and demonstrating complete recovery of life." Not only is there a serious exegetical error in interpreting Jesus as the agent of his identification as the Son of God in the "display of divine spiritual supremacy" and in "demonstrating complete recovery of life" (when in reality God is the primary agent), but the rendering of "Lord" by "Superior and Administrator" is entirely out of character and "by voluntarily enduring death" is an unwarranted addition.

What is even more questionable about such a translation is the fact that it so seriously fails to reflect the spirit and tone of the Epistle to the Romans. This is a letter that reveals deep personal concern for the spiritual life of the Christian community in Rome. Verbal pomposity is simply not in keeping with Paul's ministry; he purposely rejected high-sounding words, and chose to base his arguments on the power of a crucified and risen Lord. Translators must not seek to rewrite the text but to reproduce the force and the meaning of the original document, and in doing so they attempt to preserve as much of the original form as they can, insofar as that preservation does not result in serious distortion of the content.

The Dimension of Form

The dimension of form applies to the categories of transliteration, morphological structures, phrase structures, rhetorical devices, measured lines, figurative language, discourse structure, and literary genres. It may be regarded as a kind of continuum, from the most obligatory and formally conditioned to the most optional and least formally conditioned sets of features. When dealing with such a level as transliteration one does not hesitate to make rather radical adaptations, because the structures are almost entirely arbitrary and the amount of meaning carried by these formal structures is minimal. On the other hand, one does not significantly change the literary genre of a communication, because it does carry so much meaning and has far more structural parallels in different languages.

As one moves from transliteration to morphological structures, the need for adaptation becomes less, but again there is little or no hesitation to make numerous adjustments, primarily because many of the changes are obligatory and the modifications do not involve significant alterations of meaning. The same applies to the changes in phrase structure, though to a lesser extent.

The features of rhetorical devices, measured lines, and figurative language should involve somewhat less adaptation, because one attempts to preserve as much as possible their formal values—that is, their impact. Whenever changes are required, there is at least some attempt made to compensate for any loss by other or different corresponding rhetorical effects.

When one reaches the areas of discourse structure and literary genre, the need for or possibilities of adaptation are greatly reduced. Extensive alterations or transpositions must generally be rejected, because they inevitably involve significant shifts in meaning and violate the larger units of form that embody the intent of the original communication. For certain types of text and because of special features of the source and receptor languages involved, the order of features in this formal dimension may warrant certain changes. But the fundamental principle remains valid: as one proceeds from the most restricted and least meaningful structures to the most inclusive and most meaningful ones, the extent to which formal changes are advisable and necessary diminishes significantly.

5
The Content of the Message

The content of a message is what has traditionally been considered to be the meaning of the message. But since the meaning of any message is closely bound to the cultural presuppositions and values of a society, the content needs to be studied from the standpoint of the ways in which the cultures of the source and receptor languages interpret and evaluate events, objects, abstracts, and relations.

It would be wrong, however, to regard the dimension of content as merely another way of speaking about "meaning," for as already noted in Chapter 4 the various formal features of messages may also have different meanings. Of course, the content of a message does seem to be more closely related to what is generally thought of as "the meaning of an utterance." But in describing the meaning of the content, we are not talking only about the meanings of individual words or sentences, but also about the meanings of the events and objects that form integral elements of the content. In a certain sense, this is meaning on a second or higher level of significance.

For example, the literal meaning of Luke 22:52–54 is that Jesus refused to fight against or to flee from those who came to arrest him in the Garden of Gethsemane. We interpret this event (i.e., we give it a high-level meaning) as signifying Jesus' refusal to employ force. But in other cultures quite a different set of presuppositions may be applicable with quite different results. Among the Guaica of Venezuela, for instance, this type of behavior is almost unthinkable, and any Guaica man would certainly be regarded as either a coward or out of his mind not to fight back or try to escape.

Similarly, Jesus' healing of blind Bartimaeus (Mark 10:46) seems to us a marvelous blessing, but one Buddhist writer has reinterpreted this story as a curse, because after recovery of his sight the man was able to see all the ugliness and misery of human existence. Only an entirely different set of presuppositions, such as traditional Buddhism possesses, could make possible this utterly diverse high-level interpretation of the content.

From the standpoint of the difficulties faced by translators in dealing with culturally diverse features, the principal problems involve (1) zero terms, (2) figurative or illustrative events and objects, and (3) historical events and objects. The distinction between actual historical events and objects (3) and those that are merely figurative or illustrative (2) is an important distinction to make in dealing with the Bible, because so much emphasis in the Scriptures is upon God's specific acts in history. For example, the reference to the ass

48

that spoke to Balaam (Numb. 22:28–30) is far more important as an element of content than the figurative reference to an ass in the description of Issachar, "strong as an ass" (Gen. 49:14).

By the same token, a difference of weighting must be given to events and objects that have special religious importance in contrast with those that are essentially secular. For example, sacrifice has far more relevance for the biblical message than the type of community leadership based on a self-perpetuating group of elders.

On the basis of these different types of content and their relative weighting in the system of priorities, the following outline may represent the principal features of the content:

1. Specific historical events with religious significance
2. Historical events and general patterns of behavior without special religious significance
3. Figurative or illustrative events and objects
4. Proper names: persons and geographical objects
5. New borrowings for cultural specialties

In the case of the formal features discussed in Chapter 4, it seems best to begin with those instances in which modifications could most readily be made, and to proceed step by step to those formal structures that involve the greatest difficulties in making alterations. In the case of content, however, it seems better to begin with those features that can be least changed, and then to proceed to those that may be most readily altered.

Specific Historical Events with Religious Significance

Despite the fact that certain historical events in the Scriptures may give rise to considerable misunderstanding, as the result of quite different sets of cultural presuppositions about their validity and meaning, the translator is not in a position to alter what the original text has described as having taken place. For example, the fact that Jesus was circumcised on the eighth day after his birth is interpreted in some societies as being not only a hideously cruel way to treat a newborn baby but also as being quite senseless, because circumcision is thought to be applicable only to boys who have reached puberty. As a fertility cult practice, circumcision is regarded as being symbolically relevant, but as an operation to be performed upon infants, it is incomprehensible.

Though translators cannot change the events of the biblical account, they should put in some marginal note to explain something of the significance of circumcision as a rite to designate participation in God's covenant made with Israel. Cross-references to other passages in Scripture where circumcision is mentioned and explained may be helpful, and it is especially useful to have some brief word of explanation in an index or glossary.

But not every occurrence of the word "circumcision" must be treated as a specific reference to a historical event. For example, in some contexts "the circumcision" is a reference to "the Jews" and should usually be so translated. In other contexts, a phrase such as "circumcised in heart" may be rendered as "prepared in heart" or "dedicated in heart." In these contexts the terms "circumcision" or "circumcised" are used in a figurative sense, and there is not the same constraint to treat them in the same way as when circumcision refers to a specific historical event.

Some specific events may be regarded by some persons as being without special religious significance, whereas others see in them important religious implications. Jesus' making of wine at the wedding in Cana is just such an event. But whether or not one interprets this event as prefiguring Holy Communion, what is important is that the details of the event be accurately represented. One cannot, in the interests of the temperance movement, insist that Jesus made "unfermented grape juice" rather than "wine." The attempts by some to maintain that the wine spoken of in the New Testament was simply hot water poured over raisins cannot be justified by linguistic, historical, or archeological evidence.

Historical Events and General Patterns of Behavior without Special Religious Significance

In addition to the numerous specific historical events having important religious significance, there are numerous general patterns of behavior that have certain religious implications, but they may seem perverse, unreasonable, or senseless when viewed from the standpoint of the presuppositions of some receptor cultures. For example, in some societies lepers are not excluded from normal interpersonal relations, and hence the biblical accounts about exclusion of lepers seem totally inhuman. In order for readers to understand certain of the regulations involving lepers, it is important that some marginal or glossary note be given to explain the biblical viewpoint. The "uncleanness" of menstruating women is likewise subject to serious questioning in societies that regard menstruation as a symbol of fertility and not as a sign of "untouchableness." Similarly, prohibitions concerning certain foods as being "unclean" seem especially arbitrary and meaningless in societies where persons have thrived as a result of eating just such foods.

Accordingly, some explanation in a glossary and ample cross-referencing may be necessary to help the reader understand the presuppositions underlying the biblical account. But in none of these instances should the translator change the text to accommodate it to the viewpoint of the receptor culture. The translator must represent consistently the biblical point of view, because it is part of the total cultural framework of the Bible.

Though certain specific historical events may not involve important themes of the biblical message, one is not in a position to change the character of such events as they are described in the biblical account. Michal's taunting of David for having danced naked before the Lord (2 Sam. 6:20) cannot be altered so as to make him dance in his underwear, as one translator wanted to do. One may wish to question whether Balaam's ass actually spoke, but the faithful translator is not going to change the passage so as to imply that Balaam merely thought his ass was speaking, when all the time it was only his guilty conscience.

Some historical events seem to have obvious meanings to us, but to persons in other cultures they may be quite meaningless. When Pilate called for water to wash his hands and thus symbolized his unwillingness to accept responsibility for the death of Jesus, we readily see the significance of the act (washing away the stain of guilt), but in other cultures such a practice may seem senseless. Accordingly, some explanatory note may be required to make clear the meaning of Pilate's action.

Similarly, the casting of lots, referred to frequently in the Scriptures, is entirely unknown in some receptor cultures, and this may require some kind of marginal explanation.

In some instances translators have been reluctant to employ biblical descriptions of events because they seemed to imply contrary meanings. For example, the prediction of Jesus "coming in the clouds" can have quite a different meaning in some parts of the Orient where a person associated with clouds would be a "troublemaker." Similarly, in India some translators have argued that it might be better to say that Abraham killed a fat sheep for the heavenly visitors rather than a calf, because there is such a widespread prejudice against the eating of beef. But one cannot introduce such cultural adjustments into a text without running the risk of distorting the account.

Some persons are not so concerned about the events in the text of the Scriptures as they are about some of the events that are not specifically noted. For example, in Mark 9:14 the text says that the teachers of the law were arguing with the disciples. One editor insisted that the translators should indicate what the argument was all about. Furthermore, he wanted to know what the teachers of the law were doing there in the first place. In addition, the disciples did not answer Jesus' question, "What are you arguing with them about?" The editor insisted that some reply should be inserted.

These, however, are features of events that the writer did not choose to communicate, and a translator of the Bible is not in a position to insert them. In the first place, we do not know what Mark would have inserted had he thought it relevant to do so, but what is important is that he evidently did not regard such information as essential to his purpose, and so omitted it. The translator must do the same. In any account of an event there are always a number of elements that could be added, for no description is ever complete. Selection is one of the essential features of any discourse, and though translators may not agree with what the original writer regarded as worth recording, they are nevertheless bound to accept the limitations of the original writer's selection. Selection is always the author's prerogative.

In some instances, however, there may be some problems in the progression of thought that can be succinctly remedied, without unwarranted addition of information. For example, the statement in Acts 1:13, "They entered Jerusalem and went up to the room where they were staying," seems quite confusing in some languages, because it would imply that Jerusalem was some sort of building, or that the town was a collection of rooms rather than of houses. Therefore, it may be more natural to say, "They entered the city of Jerusalem and went up to the room of a house where they had been staying." This type of supplementation by so-called classifiers, such as "city" and "house," is quite different from the insertion of entirely new information.

The Parable of the Sower is quite meaningful to many persons in the western world, but it can be utterly confusing to persons who are not acquainted with broadcast sowing. Where only planting with dibble sticks is known, it seems inconceivable that one would attempt to grow anything on a path, or that anyone would expect plants to grow when there was not sufficient depth of soil. The folly of throwing seed onto a path, over rocky ground, or among thorn bushes so confuses some readers that they do not see the point of the story. On the other hand, one cannot eliminate the process of sowing and substitute planting, for then the parable would lose most of its significance. For this parable one must retain broadcast sowing, but it may be necessary to explain the nature of such a process. In many instances it is very useful to have a picture of someone engaged in such sowing. Even this will not always convince receptors that the practice described in the Bible is sensible (most persons think that foreigners have strange and inefficient ways of doing things anyway), but it will provide some basis for understanding the parable.

For some cultures it may be necessary to explain somewhat fully the presence of "flute players" (or "musicians") at a funeral (Matt. 9:23), because in some societies this could mean that the "mourners" were apparently delighted that the child had died. Some marginal note may also be necessary to explain the importance of the "gate" of the city, not as a means for entering and leaving, but as the center for business, legal procedures, and the meetings of the elders, equivalent in other cultures to "the town square" or "the central plaza."

References to the use of sackcloth and ashes as symbols of mourning almost always require some explanation, and the prohibition of "boiling a kid in its mother's milk" (Deut. 14:21) may be given some meaning by explaining that this was apparently a reference to a fertility cult practice. For some societies, the stern admonition against Jews intermarrying with foreigners is understandable, because many societies practice a form of endogamous marriage—that is, marriage only within a prescribed social group. But for other peoples the rigid restrictions against marrying foreigners living within the same region may require some explanation and cross-referencing.

When a translation involves historical events (whether specific or general —that is, whether as particular events or as recurring patterns of behavior) that have meanings that may be misleading or confusing, it is important that some marginal help be provided, so that the reader may be able to understand better how the original receptors of the message understood the events in question. Translators cannot alter the events, but by a judicious use of classificatory identification in the text and by supplementary information, whether in the margin, index, glossary, or cross-references, they can provide some basis for more satisfactory comprehension.

Figurative or Illustrative Events and Objects

In contrast with the treatment of actual historical events, the handling of figurative or illustrative reference to events and objects involves somewhat different principles and procedures of translation. As noted above, specific reference to the act of circumcision must be introduced when the text speaks of a particular person being circumcised. But when a purely figurative use of "circumcision" is involved, it is possible to shift the figure to a nonfigurative equivalent, especially when the original figure does not make sense in a receptor language.

Similarly, in passages that speak of blood being poured on the altar, the literal substance must be referred to, but in passages in which the Scriptures speak of a Christian being "saved by his blood," one may translate "saved by his death" or "saved by his sacrificial death," since "blood" is a figurative substitute for "death." Some persons, however, feel that the term "blood" has such important religious connotations because of its relationship to the sacrificial system that it should be retained at all costs and therefore one should employ "saved by Christ shedding his own blood."

There may be significant differences of opinion as to the figurative nature of certain terms in particular contexts. For example, in Genesis 1 some persons have insisted that "day" be translated as "eon" in view of present-day geological evidence. But this makes any reference to "the seventh day" irrelevant. Accounts such as Genesis 1 must be made internally consistent, even though on a higher level one may desire to interpret such a passage as being symbolic.

As in the case of historical events, there may be differences of opinion as to the extent of religious symbolism or significance in certain figurative uses. For example, "take this cup from me" (Luke 22:42) may be understood merely as "save me from this experience" or "do not allow me to undergo this suffering," but some persons see in the use of "cup" an allusion to the Eucharist, and therefore they feel that the symbol of "cup" should be retained. If necessary, some explanation could be added in a footnote or in the text by translating "cup" as "cup of suffering."

Expressions used in vows—for example, "as God lives" (2 Sam. 2:27) and "before God" (Gal. 1:20)—may be regarded as figurative expressions with special religious significance, and their rendering in receptor languages may differ appreciably. For example, in 2 Samuel 2:27 one may wish to employ "as surely as God is alive" or "as certain as God exists," or even "I make my promise before God himself" or "God himself is hearing what I say, and therefore you may be sure it is true." In Galatians 1:20 the last rendering would also be appropriate, because Paul is making a strong affirmation. But to render it literally as "so help me God," may be misleading when used with the phrase, "I am not lying."

Because of the obvious differences between cultures in matters of ecology and artifacts, many persons conclude that translation is impossible. Should one say "white as snow" to persons who do not know about snow, and should one say "white as wool" when the only wool known is a dirty gray or brown? When Jesus insists that new cloth should not be put on an old garment, this may seem exceedingly strange in areas where this is a very normal practice. In fact, clothes may be so covered with patches that it is almost impossible to determine what was the original cloth of the garment.

In reality, however, these problems of figurative or illustrative meaning are not so complex as might be assumed, and there are several types of solutions, depending upon the extent of formal and functional parallelism in corresponding objects and events (i.e., between the source and receptor cultures) and upon the existing usage within the particular receptor language.

The first type of adaptation in form involves a shift from the more specific to the more generic form or meaning. For example, there may be no millstones in a culture, but one can always speak of "tying a heavy stone to his neck and dropping him into the sea." In the case of "white as snow," one can employ a nonfigurative generic expression such as "very very white." And the idiom "I will take my flesh in my teeth" (Job 13:14) may become "I am ready to risk my life." The phrase "gird the loins of your mind" (1 Peter 1:13) may be rendered as "have your minds ready for action." "Wash the feet of the saints" may be translated as "be hospitable to fellow believers," but in this idiom there may also be the feature of "humble service." Of course, in John 13:5 where Jesus washes the disciples' feet one cannot employ any such generic statement, because in this context the reference is to a specific event.

In certain cases a literal translation is impossible because of special symbolic values associated with certain cultural objects. For example, in Balinese the viper is regarded as a snake of paradise, and hence "generation of vipers" (Matt. 3:7, 12:34, 23:33; Luke 3:7) would scarcely be a denunciation. However, it is possible to communicate the meaning of this phrase by substituting a more generic term—for example, "vermin."

In some instances it is possible to preserve a figurative usage, even though it may seem strange, by identifying its function with some added generic expression. For example, "anointing my head with oil" (Ps. 23:5) may be translated as "welcomed me by anointing my head with oil." In other contexts, however, "anointing with oil" may be rendered simply as "to appoint" or "to commission," if this is the meaning in the context. One may, however, wish to preserve something of the original expression and add what might be called a defining classifier—for example, "appoint by putting oil on his head."

Another way of dealing with figurative expressions that are not comprehensible in the receptor language is to shift them from metaphors to similes. In place of "Judah is a young lion" (Gen. 49:9), one may have "Judah is just like a young lion." "You are the salt of the earth" (Matt. 5:13) may be rendered as "you are just like salt for all humankind."

When the object or event in the source-language text is relatively similar in form and function to a corresponding object or event in the culture of the receptor language, one can often substitute one for the other. For example, in some parts of Africa the "royal stool" is equivalent to a "throne," and "snow" may be spoken of as "frost." Similarly, "wolf" may be translated as "jackal" or "hyena-like animal" in some contexts. In certain regions "yoke" in some contexts is equivalent to "tumpline" (a special braided band that goes across the forehead and is used to carry heavy loads), but in other parts of the world the closest equivalent is "carrying stick." These terms are quite appropriate in translating "yoke" in Matthew 11:29, but would, of course, be quite impossible in talking about "yokes" used with oxen, in which case some descriptive equivalent as well as marginal note may be required.

There are, however, a number of problems that can arise in making certain substitutions. If the objects only have functional parrallelism and lack all formal resemblance, one may encounter strong objections, especially from better educated receptors who will insist that the translation is not correct. For example, some translators have used "wild boar" for "lion," and though in certain figurative contexts this might be acceptable, it involves problems elsewhere. For example, Judah as a "wild boar" (Gen. 49:9) involves the problem of clean and unclean animals, with all the accompanying associations.

One translator substituted "horse" for "sheep" in a translation made for horse-loving Indians of Canada, but missionary colleagues strongly objected and the Indians completely rejected such a usage as being paternalistic. In areas where camels are unknown some translators have attempted to substitute the water buffalo, but to do this consistently results in nonsense, because both in form and ecological setting it is difficult to conceive of two animals more unlike than the camel and the water buffalo. When the forms and functions of objects are too divergent, it is much better to shift figurative to nonfigurative expressions or to borrow terms (especially if they are required in other contexts that are not figurative) and explain them in a glossary.

There are situations, however, in which figurative expressions in one language can be matched quite successfully by corresponding figurative expressions in another language. For example, the description of Judah's wealth being so great that he could "wash his clothes in wine" (Gen. 49:11) has a close parallel in Shilluk as "wash his clothes in oil." Of course, these expressions are not to be understood literally in either Hebrew or Shilluk; it is only an idiomatic way of describing wealth through conspicuous and wasteful consumption.

In Acts 7:54, the clause "they gnashed at him with their teeth" is understood in some languages to imply literally "chewing on him." One may sometimes find a parallel idiom, as in Yao, "they had itchy teeth," meaning they were anxious to destroy him. The idiom "thou hast stripped off my sackcloth" (Ps. 30:11) may be changed in the Bamileke language to "you have taken the bag of mourning from my hand," because in Bamileke society women in mourning normally carry a raffia bag slung over the arm. This does not mean, however, that in all contexts "sackcloth" can be translated as "bag of mourning." It is only that in certain figurative contexts the closely parallel figure is acceptable.

To some extent the acceptability of substitute figures of speech depends upon the cultural views on literal correspondence. For example, in Balinese there seems to be no reason not to translate 2 Timothy 2:4 by "no warrior carries a market bag" as a figurative rendering of the more prosaic expression "get mixed up in the affairs of civilian life." But in some languages there would be serious question about translating Matthew 23:24 ("strain out a gnat and swallow a camel") by "brush away the chaff, but leave a dead cow in the water pond." The two expressions are functional equivalents, but they represent such entirely different sets of circumstances that persons who are at all culturally insecure are likely to insist that the translator has distorted the text.

The rendering of "I will take my flesh in my teeth" (Job 13:14) by "I will put my neck in the noose" (NEB) is much more acceptable, because it does not seem to be such a wide departure nor to depend too much upon local cultural specialties. That is to say, the cultural practice of hanging was not unknown in biblical times.

When there is a strong literalist tendency in a culture, and especially in circumstances in which such a tendency has been strongly reinforced by certain types of teaching concerning the Bible, one must be quite cautious about introducing substitute figures. When they are employed in order to make sense of an otherwise meaningless or even misleading expression, it may be useful to put in the margin a literal rendering of the source-language phrase.

Proper Names

The treatment of proper names may seem out of place in this section, which deals with content, because it is precisely a lack of content that characterizes such names. Nevertheless, the evident lack of content can produce a number of problems, either because of accidental resemblances or because such terms had much more significance in their "home language" than in the receptor language.

In the borrowing of proper names, one must always be alert to the possibility that the transliterated form will actually resemble a receptor-language word, with a meaning that may be quite unacceptable. If this is the case, some slight adjustment in the form of the name must be made in order that any wrong interpretation of a name may be avoided.

The translator must be aware, however, that especially in Hebrew names often did carry important connotative meanings, and in fact were often given to persons either in commemoration of some event associated with their birth or as a prediction concerning their future roles. It is particularly important that this supplementary information be given whenever the meaning of a passage depends upon the literal etymology of a name. In some instances, the text itself supplies such data, but more often than not the relations are not sufficiently specific, and the explanations of the text must be supplemented by some marginal helps. See, for example, the typical marginal notes on *Adam, Cain, Abel, Seth, Abraham, Jacob, Esau,* and *Ishmael.*

In some cultures the meaning of names is so evident and such an important feature of the culture that some missionary translators have concluded that it might be best to translate all names that have presumably clear etymologies. Accordingly, instead of transliterating Jacob as a proper name, an indigenous term meaning "cheater" would be employed as his name. But this is not a legitimate practice. In the first place, it makes too sharp a distinction between names that have etymologies and those that do not. Secondly, it would suggest that the biblical characters were themselves members of the local receptor-language society, rather than belonging to quite a different culture. And thirdly, the name would constantly refer to a relation or a role rather than to the particular person and thus tend to distort the function of the name.

When there are variant forms of a person's name or different names for the same person, the variant forms should be reproduced in a single one. For example, there is sometimes confusion in Hebrew between the letters *d* and *r,* with the result that the same person may at one time be called by a name having the letter *d* and in other contexts by the form of the same name having the letter *r.* Also, Old Testament persons referred to in the New Testament should have the same form of name in both places. For example, it is unnecessarily confusing to speak of "Elijah" in the Old Testament and "Elias" in the New Testament.

It may be extremely useful to employ classifiers with geographical proper names, especially at points of first occurrence in a text or in first translations. One may speak of "City Jerusalem" rather than merely "Jerusalem" and "River Jordan" instead of simply "Jordan." The use of such classifiers does not mean adding any information to the text itself. It is only a means of helping the new reader to understand something of the meaning of the zero words.

Quite frequently it is possible to translate the generic portions of certain place designations and thus accomplish the result of having classifiers. For example, Kiriath-arba may be rendered as Arba City and Kiriath-jearim may be rendered as Jearim City. In other instances it is possible to use a translation of a proper name that may be even more meaningful. For example, Ramathlehi may be rendered as "Jawbone Hill" and Allon-bacuth as "Oak of Weeping."

New Borrowings for Cultural Specialities

If one borrows a term for "camel," it may be possible to add a classifier in the form "an animal called camel." This immediately tells the reader that this is an animal, and in a number of contexts this is about all that is necessary (e.g., Mark 1:6). For all such new borrowings it is essential to have some descriptive statement in a glossary or index, and in cases like "camel" it is extremely useful to introduce a picture.

In the borrowing of terms such as "ruby," "amethyst," "topaz," and the like, one may also employ classifiers—for example, "precious stone called ruby" or "ruby jewel." It is also possible in a context such as Revelation 21:19-20 to translate as "all kinds of valuable stones," and then employ designations of color, provided the receptor language has terms that are sufficiently precise. The actual form of the names could then be introduced in the margin, if this is thought to be necessary.

In the introduction of new borrowings, one must always be aware of terms that may already exist in the language, either indigenous terms or other previous borrowings of the same or a similar term. In one language in the Philippines a term for "wolf" was borrowed from Spanish in the form of *lobo,* but another term, the Spanish *globo* ("ball"), had already been borrowed and had undergone a change in form from *globo* to *lobo.* Speakers of this language could assume that in the New Testament "balls covered with a sheep skin" made better sense than "wolves covered with a sheep skin," especially inasmuch as *lobo* in the meaning of "ball" was well known and *lobo* in the meaning of "wolf" was rare.

In order to avoid borrowings some translators have employed descriptive equivalents. These may be very useful. For example, an "anchor" may be "a heavy piece of iron to keep the ship from moving" and a "tent" may be "a dwelling made of cloth."

6
The Discovery and Analysis of Problems

Perhaps the most important aspect in finding satisfactory solutions to problems involving form and content is to become aware of the difficulties. Most problems remain unsolved because translators are not fully sensitive to them. In fact, awareness usually means that the problem is at least half-solved. But being conscious of problems of form and content depends very much upon the background and mental attitudes of translators.

Differences in Cultural Backgrounds of Translators

With respect to awareness of translational difficulties, Bible translators may generally be placed in four classes, involving two sets of parallel sub-classes, one set being applicable to missionaries and another to nationals. Obviously, any complete classification would have to take into account several degrees of difference within each class, but this rough classification is adequate for the purpose of calling attention to certain problems.

Missionary translators differ very much in their sensitivity to translational problems. This does not depend primarily upon the extent of their knowledge of the source-language texts and culture (though there may be rather striking differences at this point also), but essentially upon their degree of cultural identification with the receptor language and culture. If they have a negative valuation of the receptor people (including both their language and their culture), they are very likely to be blind to the problems of communication, for they tend to regard anything indigenous as being "blighted by sin" or "under the dominion of Satan." On the other hand, some missionaries are so romantic about the exotic features of the language and culture in which they are working that they want to preserve everything at any cost.

The missionary translator who avoids romanticizing the receptor language and repudiates harsh negative valuations and paternalism in judging the receptor language-culture will be in a much better position to recognize the real problems of communication between the source and receptor languages and to find adequate solutions.

National translators also fall into two classes: those who exhibit insecurity with respect to their own language and those who do not. National translators who have been "alienated" from their own culture often encounter great difficulties in finding proper solutions to translation problems. Having been educated almost exclusively in a foreign language and generally having assumed the superiority of the culture associated with this foreign language, such translators tend to be even more prejudiced against the receptor language than are most foreign missionaries. Because such translators are far more likely to think in the foreign language than in their own mother tongue, they may quite unconciously carry over many ideas more or less word for word into their mother tongue, without realizing that they are really unnatural forms of expression. Moreover, it is often difficult for such persons to accept advice from their compatriots who have limited formal education in the language in which the translators themselves have been trained.

There are some national translators, however, who may have been alienated from their own culture at an earlier time, but who have for one reason or another completely reversed their attitudes, even to the extent that they romanticize their own indigenous backgrounds as much as some amateur linguists do. Such persons often insist on ridding their own language of borrowings and of repudiating any and all expressions that do not fit perfectly within the indigenous system of presuppositions. As a result, they find it almost impossible to translate the Bible, because it is essential that certain quite new ideas be expressed in the translation. Furthermore, these ideas inevitably run counter to many traditional concepts. It is normally not necessary to import new words, but certain new ideas must be introduced, and this may be difficult for certain persons to accept.

On the other hand, most national translators have a good balance of knowledge and judgment. Their knowledge of the source-language documents may be limited, and to make up for this deficiency they need commentaries and books on biblical backgrounds. Furthermore, a missionary may also play an important role as a resource person, providing such translators with important supplementary information.

Though most national translators have an excellent grasp of their own language, their knowledge is often not systematic. They know what sounds right, but they often do not know why this is so. They know all the pieces of the cultural puzzle, but they have never thought about putting the puzzle together. Hence, they may not understand all the implications of some renderings, not having thought much about the why's and wherefore's of their own patterns of life.

Extremes in the Introduction of Adjustments in Form and Content

The traditional view of some is that only persons of liberal theological views are likely to "tamper" with the Scriptures, and therefore to guarantee accuracy and fidelity to the Word of God one must make certain that Bible translators are theologically conservative. Though such reasoning may seem to be quite justified, the actual situation is often quite different.

It is true that some translators with strongly liberal tendencies have undertaken to transpose certain sections of the text on the basis of presumed divergencies of source, and in some instances certain translators have even introduced their own interpretations of demon possession, miracles, and other phenomena that they may regard as being contrary to the presuppositions of modern times. But theologically conservative persons have also made translations with radical transpositions of the text, usually in the interests of what they regard as being "more consistent." Some, for example, have changed the wording of Mark at points so that it would agree better with John and have introduced into the text certain background explanations, which, though perfectly true, are not part of the original text.

The motivations for such changes may have all been quite worthy, for they are usually made in the name of "improving the text" and "making it more intelligible to the natives." But such "improvements" often reveal a rather shallow view of revelation, and evangelistic concerns to make the text more readable have often arisen from underestimating the capacities of receptors. As a result, receptor-language persons who have acquired some education have frequently come to repudiate the intentions of the translators as being nothing less than pernicious paternalism.

In contrast with the tendency to go too far in making formal and cultural transpositions in the text, a number of translators have not gone far enough in making legitimate adjustments to the requirements of receptor languages. But again this is not the exclusive fault of theologically conservative persons, as is so often intimated. Though it is true that some theologically conservative translators have thought that they must translate almost word for word, even to the point of making a fetish out of "concordant translating" (with the result that their texts are sometimes quite misleading to readers), there are some theologically liberal translators who are almost equally insistent upon preserving the verbal forms of the original texts. Such persons view the rigid adherence to the features of form and content as being essential if one is to preserve the mystery of language, to provide a basis for "liturgical atmosphere," and to retain the historical setting.

These translators seem to be more interested in creating emotional attitudes than in communicating a message, and in satisfying certain psychological needs of adherents rather than in challenging nonbelievers with the present-day relevance of the Good News. But despite one's judgment as to the validity of such an approach to translation, one must recognize that extreme literalism is by no means a monopoly of those who are strongly conservative in theological outlook, nor is radical recasting of the text the dominant tendency of those who are theologically liberal.

Perhaps one of the principal reasons for lack of balance and judgment in the extent to which adjustments in form can and should be made results from a failure to carry out a translation program in close cooperation with an existing Christian constituency. Too often translators work in isolation from a believing community and without sufficient regard for what receptors want or expect in a translation. Such a translation is then published and often promoted with high-pressure tactics, with the result that receptors are often more confused than instructed.

The Bible translator's task is not primarily to work *for* the church but *with* the church, for even as the Scriptures first arose as a response to the needs of a believing community so a translation should reflect this same type of involved concern.

Background in the Form and Content of the Source Language

Though many Bible translators possess an excellent background (not only in a knowledge of the source languages, both Greek and Hebrew, but also in their understanding of the cultural patterns of behavior and the corresponding presuppositions), there are many whose knowledge is quite limited. For persons who do not know but who recognize that they do not know, there is always hope, for there are numerous books available to help translators. It is true that many of these books are rather technical in nature, and translators may have to read a good deal before they come upon the precise information they need. It is for this very reason that an extensive program for the preparation of translation handbooks and guides on various books of the Bible has been undertaken.

For persons who do not know about biblical backgrounds, but who think that they do, there is very little hope, for they proceed to translate with little or no awareness of the errors that they are introducing into the translation. This is largely because they have never taken the time to compare systematically the biblical presuppositions with those that they have assimilated from their own religious background or with those that belong to the receptor culture.

If one is interested in obtaining further background in the source culture, there are essentially two types of helps: (1) commentaries, which treat exegetical problems in a critical and detailed manner (homiletical commentaries are of very little help in this regard), and (2) books on general backgrounds, including biblical handbooks, encyclopedias, and such useful guides as G. Ernest Wright's *Biblical Archaeology*, R. de Vaux's *Ancient Israel, Its Life and Institutions*, and Gaalyah Cornfield's *Archeology of the Bible: Book by Book*.

Background in the Receptor-Language Culture

It is far easier to obtain relevant information on biblical backgrounds than to acquire corresponding information on the receptor-language culture. Because of the manner in which information from commentaries is normally supplied—namely, at that point in the text where it is significant—the translator can usually have available the kind of data needed to understand the cultural backgrounds of a particular biblical passage. This is by no means true of information on the receptor-language culture. This information has to be gathered in quite different ways and systematically studied before it is normally applicable to particular problems.

One may have the help of some unusually intelligent and perceptive national colleagues who are able to provide the necessary information, but such an ideal situation is quite rare. Translators are far more likely to need to study the culture in some objective and systematic way, because only then can they apply the necessary information at the right time.

Such an approach may seem required for a missionary, but scarcely necessary for a national translator who is expected to know his own culture. The difficulty is that often national translators may have only a superficial knowledge of their own culture, usually because they have been educated away from it. But even if national translators have lived all their life within their own culture, their knowledge of their own culture may be so unsystematic and piecemeal that they cannot readily see the distinctive differences between the local patterns of behavior and those mentioned in the Scriptures.

National translators may, for example, be convinced that children born of incest never attain maturity, but the story of Lot and his two daughters, whose offspring became the patriarchs of Moab and Ammon, never seems to be in conflict with the indigenous beliefs, largely because the whole setting of the biblical account appears to be so distant and foreign. Similarly, they may know that in contrast with the steep, thatched roofs of the local area the houses of biblical times were largely flat-topped and made of timbers, brush, and pounded dirt, but they seldom stop to think how difficult it is for persons in the receptor culture to understand the story of men letting the paralytic down through the roof of the house where Jesus was living. Likewise, they may read the account of Absalom having intercourse with David's concubines, without realizing that this can have quite a different meaning for persons of their own culture.

In order to acquire some appreciation for the structures of a culture, a translator needs to become familiar with certain of the general treatments of anthropology, especially those written from the more popular standpoint— for example, Clyde Kluckhohn, *Mirror for Man* (New York: McGraw-Hill Book Company, 1949) and Eugene A. Nida, *Customs and Cultures* (Pasadena, California: Carey Library, 1954). In order to appreciate something of the new dimensions in an ethnography, in which the members of an indigenous people are treated as real persons and not merely as parts of social structures, one may wish to read Kenneth E. Read, *The High Valley* (New York: Charles Scribner's Sons, 1965).

If further study and deeper analysis is required, one may wish to pursue some systematic investigation of the local culture following *Notes and Queries*, published by the Royal Anthropological Institute of Great Britain. But there is no substitute for continued association with real persons and participation in the local society. This means tireless observation and intelligent questions. But not such questions as "What does that mean?" or "Why do you do that?" Far more meaningful are such questions as "How often do you do that?" "Who normally also does this?" "What advantage is it for you to do that?" All such investigations must constantly distinguish between the real and the ideal reasons for behavior and the real and ideal presuppositions that underlie different attitudes and values.

Perhaps even more important than technical knowledge of a culture is an alert imagination, one that can see the ridiculous in an expression and can discover why persons secretly laugh at what has been said. One must be able to imagine how persons are going to respond to a phrase such as "lift up your eyes." Will it mean to pick them up off a table (as it did in one language of the Middle East) or to roll them back into the head in a trance (as in one language of the Orient)? Is likening Issachar to a wild ass (Gen. 49:14) a compliment or an insult? When one declares "the Lord is my rock" is that a help or an obstacle? And does the clause "he ties his young donkey to a grapevine and washes his garments in wine" (Gen. 49:11) mean that Judah is a fool or so rich that he can afford such a wasteful practice?

As one learns more about the biblical culture and the receptor culture and has occasion to study and compare similarities and differences, a very important development takes place. At first, one is almost inevitably impressed with the differences between cultures, but gradually one begins to see more and more similarities and to discover beneath the surface of the divergencies many features that cultures have in common. These are essentially the universals or near universals of culture that make possible communication within and between languages.

Textual Features Indicative of Underlying Problems

As one examines any text to be translated into another language, there are certain features that immediately suggest that there may be certain underlying problems involved in reproducing its meaning in a receptor language. The following series includes some of the most common features that cause difficulties:

1. *Idioms.* Inasmuch as idioms tend to be reflections of highly specific cultural features, they are very likely to cause complications in translation. An expression such as "upon Edom I cast my shoe" (Ps. 60:8) must be carefully analyzed and its meaning fully determined before any attempt can be made to translate it, for the idiom refers to possession of land, not rejection of it.

2. *Figurative meanings.* Figurative meanings of single words differ from idioms in that the figurative extension of meaning affects only one word in the phrase, but all such figurative meanings are suspect, inasmuch as they also tend to be closely bound to cultural specialties. In the phrase "to eat the fat of the land" (Gen. 45:18) the term "fat" cannot be taken in its literal meaning. This must be some reference to the "fine produce" or "the rich products" of the land.

3. *Any object that does not occur in the receptor culture.* Terms such as "lion," "camel," "mustard," "ship," and "phylactery" identify objects that are not indigenous to some cultures. This does not mean that persons do not

know about such objects or cannot learn what such objects are, but it does mean that often some assistance must be provided, so that the requisite background information can be given in a satisfactory way.

4. *Any activity that would seem strange to persons in the receptor culture.* It may seem quite strange to a people to be commanded not to sow their fields with two kinds of seeds (Lev. 19:19) when local agricultural practices have proved over centuries that mixed planting is highly beneficial. Workers who use oxen for plowing will generally agree that an ox and an ass will not plow together (Deut. 22:9), but others who are not acquainted with the use of draft animals may find such injunctions totally meaningless. Tramping out grain by means of oxen appears to many persons as very wasteful, and especially so if the oxen are not muzzled.

5. *Any implied presuppositions that may be contrary to those of the receptor culture.* The presuppositions about positive taboo associated with the Ark of the Covenant may be quite contrary to beliefs in the receptor culture.

6. *Expressions of pyschological experience.* Expressions for "love," "hate," "joy," and "pleasure" are often very closely related to some organ of the body—for example, "heart," "bowels," or "kidneys"—but there may be quite different sets of associations. For example, in the Scriptures the "heart" is primarily the center of intellectual perception and moral wisdom, rather than the focus of emotional feeling, as in most European languages.

7. *Highly generic terms.* Highly generic terms that depend primarily on conceptual, rather than perceptual, categories—for example, "power," "wisdom," "knowledge," "goodness," "evil," and "life"—must be carefully analyzed to determine whether some of the semantic components of such terms reflect special receptor-language concepts. For example, in the Scriptures "knowledge," especially in such phrases as "knowledge of God" and "knowledge of evil," refers to experience rather than to information.

8. *Linguistic forms that are quite different from those in the receptor language.* Such features as rhetorical questions, the use of "we" when the reference is to "I," and third-person imperatives (e.g., "let there be light") may pose serious complications in translation.

9. *Sequences of events in nonhistorical order.* Whenever events are given in a text in an order that is not chronological, the translator should be alert to possible and even probable difficulties. For example, in Mark 1:43 the text says that Jesus sent a leper away, while verse 44 contains the instructions that Jesus gave to the man before he had left.

10. *Poetic structures.* Poetic structures pose difficulties in selecting appropriate corresponding forms (those of the source and receptor languages are rarely, if ever, the same). And the fact that poetic structures tend to have a much higher percentage of figurative language suggests still further complications. Also the fact that poetic structures in Hebrew are so heavily parallel produces difficulties in finding similar parallel structures that will not be misleading or in compensating for loss of emphasis by the use of some equivalent devices.

11. *Larger units of discourse.* Translators tend to overlook some of the important elements in the larger units of discourse—for example, connectives (which link a unit with what has preceded and with what follows), expressions of setting (which indicate time and place), and identifications of literary genre. For example, in Greek a parable is often marked by the indefinite pronoun *tis*, which in combination with *anthropos* ("man") has often been mistranslated as "a certain man," when in fact it should be restructured in English as "there was once a man."

There are a number of other features of any text that cause difficulties for translators, but these eleven types of features are some of the most common sources of problems.

Analysis of the Function and Significance of Textual Features

It is one thing to become alert to the difficulties involved in a number of special features of form and content, but something quite different to be able to analyze satisfactorily the function and significance of such features. In ascertaining the functional significance of formal features, the translator is concerned principally with the "impact" and appropriateness to the content. Rhetorical questions certainly carry more impact than simple statements, but if the receptor language cannot employ a question in such a context, how is it possible to produce a similar impact?

Sometimes this may be done by employing a particularly strong affirmative or negative statement. At other times, one may introduce a negative rhetorical question by an appropriate phrase—for example, "No one should ever ask"—followed by the question. There are a number of other ways in which one can treat such matters. What is important is that one recognize the force of the source-language expression and on this basis determine what is the closest natural equivalent in the receptor language.

At times, however, problems of form are not merely matters of impact but involve contextual appropriateness. In this respect, poetry is a particularly sensitive formal structure. When employed in the denunciations spoken by the prophets, poetry may make the subject matter seem trivial. On the other hand, to make the Psalms so largely unreadable in public, as the American Standard Version did, is to rob them of much of their intrinsic and original value.

As a help in ascertaining the impact and appropriateness of formal features in the source text, one must look to analytical commentaries to provide answers. Unfortunately, however, many such commentaries take for granted matters of form and concentrate almost exclusively on problems of content. Nevertheless, broad reading in this field will help a translator become increasingly more sensitive to the values associated with formal features.

It is also useful to read what professional translators have written on problems of translating literary works. *On Translation*, edited by Reuben A. Brower (Cambridge: Harvard University Press, 1960) is very useful, and *Style in*

Language, edited by Thomas A. Sebeok (Cambridge: MIT Press, 1960) can also be helpful in making one more sensitive to some of the difficulties involved in literary translation. In French the book edited by E. Cary and R.W. Jumpelt, *La qualité en matière de traduction* (New York: The Macmillan Company, 1963) is an excellent summary of views on translation, and in German the volume by Fritz Güttinger, *Zielsprache* (Zürich: Manesse Verlag, 1963) is particularly effective in dealing with important issues in literary translation. See also the Selected Bibliography below.

In order to determine what is likely to be the most appropriate corresponding form in a receptor language, one cannot depend upon analyses based only on features of the source language. Rather, one must base one's judgment upon certain essential principles of translation, which have been formulated in such books as *Bible Translating, Toward a Science of Translating, Theory and Practice of Translation,* and *Language Structure and Translation*, all of which focus primary attention upon the problems of finding satisfactory equivalents in various receptor languages.

For techniques involved in ascertaining the meaning of the cultural content of the Scriptures and how receptors in other language-culture contexts are likely to react to them, perhaps the most comprehensive analysis is to be found in *Exploring Semantic Structures*, where the various analytical procedures are carefully described and illustrated. For the translator who is primarily concerned with the difficulties of meaning arising from cultural specialities, and especially from features of content that have special symbolic significance, one may summarize the relevant procedure as a process of determining those features of the object or event that serve to set it off from all other similar or related objects or events. In other words, one must determine the "necessary and sufficient" features of any object or event so as to distinguish it from any other.

For example, the shaking of hands may be described as having three essential components: (1) two persons extend right hands toward each other (though usually one person takes the initiative in the act), (2) the hands are clasped, and (3) hands (and arms) are moved up and down one or more times before being released.

There are, of course, a number of special features about shaking hands that are applicable to certain situations. For example, it is usually the person in the superior role who first extends the hand, though in the expression of thanks it is the recipient of benefits who initiates the extension of the hands. Hands may be firmly clasped or only gently touched, depending upon the degree of intimacy of the persons, the frequency with which they have met, and the formality of the occasion. Finally, the shaking may be vigorous or weak, the muscle tone may be strong or limp, and the action may be extended or abruptly terminated, depending also upon a number of factors, including the sex of the participants, the type of occasion, and the physical and emotional state of the participants.

But even describing all the formal features of handshaking does not mean that one has dealt with the cultural meaning of the process. In fact, the various meanings are almost always more complex than the features of the act itself. The shaking of hands may signify that friends have met again after some period of absence, or it may be that persons who have not previously met each other are just being introduced (in which case, the handshaking is conspicuously less vigorous). Handshaking can also be employed to conclude an agreement, to express thanks for a favor, and to say goodbye.

As in the case of almost any communication system, handshaking can be used to communicate intents that are not in keeping with the overt forms. For example, it is possible for the host to speed up the departure of his guest by taking the initiative in shaking hands. This is a particularly well developed device used by businesspeople who want to get rid of applicants or salespeople. Such handshaking preserves the form of friendliness, while at the same time indicating clearly that the person's presence is no longer desirable. In the same way one can exclaim, "We do love to have you so much," while intonational contours and the tone of voice communicate precisely the opposite—namely, "Frankly, we hate to have you around."

If one were to make a careful study of all the various forms of handshaking employed in the western world and the ways in which they communicate meanings, the results would certainly fill a book, so complex and involved is this one pattern of culture. In other societies similar kinds of activities may be equally complex. The ways in which persons in some West African tribes meet and snap fingers carry equally complex messages. Hence, it is inadvisable to take for granted a particular element in a given culture and assume that it always has a single meaning. In fact, seldom does any widely used pattern of behavior have only one meaning.

Circumcision certainly has a number of different meanings, though the act itself is relatively simple: (1) a surgical operation (2) involving the removal of the foreskin of the penis. But the cultural meanings are many and varied. For Jews it symbolizes identification with "the people of God," and thus carries both ethnic and religious significance. Circumcision was required, for example, for intermarriage (see Gen. 34:14–17), and it became a determinative factor in symbolizing a person's relation to the Mosaic code (circumcision was the crucial symbol for the Judaizers in the early church, see Gal. 2:3–5).

For most non-Jews in the western world, however, circumcision is only a means to guarantee a more hygienic condition, though it is true that some persons, following the lead of certain psychiatrists, tend to see a number of covert elements of father-son rivalry and conflict. In a number of other societies in the world, however, circumcision is a fertility rite associated with sexual maturity and becomes a symbol of manliness and entrance into adult society. It also has a number of other covert meanings in such societies because it is surrounded with so much secrecy, special ceremonies, and important changes in status and role.

One event that had considerable symbolic significance in biblical times, but which has lost practically all meaning in the western world, is foot washing. The original practice involved: (1) the use of water (2) to wash the feet (3) of someone else. This task was normally performed by a slave of the lowest rank, and it was not only an act of hospitality, but must have also served the useful purpose of keeping the interior of a house cleaner than would otherwise have been the case. The washing of feet came to be such a symbol of hospitality that the phrase itself seems to have lost at least something of its original significance in some contexts—for example, 1 Timothy 5:10, in which "showed hospitality to fellow believers" is a more correct rendering than "washing the feet of fellow believers." In some churches foot washing is preserved as a rite, but inasmuch as it no longer retains its earlier cultural relevance and the presuppositions associated with such an act, there is very little of the original meaning left.

In dealing with any such problems involving the content of the message, one must carefully distinguish between two levels of analysis: (1) the determination of those features that accurately define the event or object in question and (2) the description of the meaning that such a feature has in the source-language culture. One should never assume that the meaning will automatically follow from the features of the form, any more than one can safely assume that the meaning of a word will be clearly evident from the sounds that make it up.

The translator's task, however, is much more complex than simply studying the source-language features of content that have symbolic significance. Translators must also analyze the features of distinctive receptor-language objects and events to determine the extent to which the forms and meanings are parallel. They can never expect them to be identical, but they must find at least some common functional basis or reject the correspondence as being wrong and inadequate.

The translator is not in a position to alter the essential features of an object or event (except where these may be used in figurative or illustrative senses, and then only with caution), and it is precisely in the areas of lack of cultural correspondence that most of the marginal notes are of particular importance. However, without an accurate analysis of the precise differences of form and meaning, it is almost impossible to formulate satisfactory marginal helps. A book that deals systematically with these problems of the distinctive features of meaning is *Componential Analysis of Meaning*.

7
Provision of Supplementary Information

Having analyzed the translational problems that arise from a lack of correspondence in form and content, it is now essential to consider how the necessary supplementary information can be supplied. But first it may be useful to ask what are in fact the valid expectations that one should have of a translation. What can one legitimately expect of a translation? What are the limits to which a translation can go in introducing adaptations to the receptor language and culture?

Legitimate Objectives of a Translation

Basically a translation should be the closest natural equivalent of the message in the source language. This means that it cannot be a word-for-word rendering of the original, because this would result in serious distortion of the message. On the other hand, it also means that a translation cannot contain such linguistic and cultural transpositions as would skew the historical setting of the communication. Therefore, the legitimate area of translational equivalence must lie somewhere between these two extremes.

From the negative point of view, one cannot expect a wider range of persons to understand a translation than was able to comprehend the original message. In fact, a relatively narrower range will understand the translation, inasmuch as the original participants in the communication (source and receptors) shared considerable information that is not available to receptors in the second language. If some of the original receptors did not understand all the implications of the message, then one must not expect that the text of a translation can be so fully explicit as to eliminate all lack of comprehension.

In the second place, one cannot expect every part of a text to be completely comprehensible without reference to the total text. Unfortunately, some translators are so anxious for receptors to comprehend each and every verse in order, that they want to build into each passage all the information that is explicitly found in later parts of the communication. Any valid discourse must be taken as a unit, and second-language receptors must be expected to derive the meaning from it in substantially the same way as first-language receptors did, though second-language receptors may require some more explicit information, either incorporated into the text (on the basis that it is structurally implicit) or added in the margin or in an appendix (on the basis that it is essential for understanding).

70

In the third place, it is wrong to try to make a translation clearer than the author intended the original to be. If there is evidence that the original author was purposely obscure or ambiguous, then the obscurity and ambiguity should be preserved, possibly with a marginal note explaining the nature of the intended obscurity or ambiguity. If on the other hand, as is usually the case, the obscurity or ambiguity arises from scholars' failure to comprehend what the author intended, then one should, in all fairness to the intent of the author, place the most likely meaning in the text and any alternative meaning or meanings in the margin.

From the positive point of view, one may state that a translation should not be misleading to the average reader for whom it is designed. If such is the case, obviously the translator has failed in some way or other. Either the translation itself must be corrected (if the problem is essentially one of incorrect interpretation of the semantic components of the expressions used) or compensating or corrective information must be supplied in the margin (if the cultural content of the original text is misleading, as viewed from the standpoint of the presuppositions of the receptor culture).

In addition, a translation should not be a meaningless string of words, from which no reasonable meaning can be readily extracted by the average reader. Either the translation itself must be corrected, so as to more satisfactorily reflect the meaning of the original or, if the original text itself is entirely incomprehensible, then the fact that no certain meaning can be given to the passage should be indicated in a marginal note.

For example, as already noted, in Mark 9:49 the sentence "For everyone will be salted with fire" does not make sense, but since scholars themselves do not really know what it means, it is quite impossible to determine how it can be more clearly expressed. A marginal note indicating that this expression is just as obscure in the original text is entirely in order.

Furthermore, no translation should be so difficult, as the result of formal overloading, that the average reader will in all probability give up reading the text. Formal overloading, which often results from the overuse of rare and difficult combinations of words, should be subjected to systematic restructuring so that the message of the text can be comprehended by the reader at a reasonably satisfactory rate. This does not mean, however, that the rate of comprehension for a book such as the Epistle to the Hebrews should be similar to that of the Gospel of Mark. Such a leveling of the communication load would obviously not only violate the formal structure of the message, but would be out of keeping with the complexity of the content.

Types of Problems Justifying Supplementary Information

In keeping with the legitimate expectancies of a satisfactory translation, supplementary information is justified in the case of the following principal types of problems: (1) important divergencies in original texts, (2) significantly different interpretations of the text, (3) historical events that may be misleading or meaningless, (4) illustrative events, (5) figurative expressions, (6) objects that may differ in form or function, and (7) zero expressions.

Only important textual variants should be noted in any text of the Scriptures. There are thousands of minor variations in the Hebrew and Greek texts of the Scriptures, but only a few hundred of them are actually important enough to warrant inclusion in marginal notes or in some special lists of alternative readings. The importance of a textual variant depends upon two factors: (a) the traditional use of such a reading in previously published translations of the Scriptures (e.g., readings that occur in the Byzantine tradition of the Greek New Testament) and that accordingly abound in translations such as the King James Version and (b) the relative weight of textual evidence. When textual evidence is rather overwhelmingly on one side or another of a textual variation, there is no need to have this represented in a listing of variant readings, unless the passage figures prominently in a particular tradition of translations. In practical terms, this means that for the Greek New Testament published by the United Bible Societies it is unwise to introduce textual notes for alternative readings if the text followed has a rating of A or B, unless the alternative represents the Textus Receptus and figures prominently in the tradition of the church.

Significantly different interpretations of the text should also be noted as supplementary information. Such alternative renderings are not only due the reader but are one aspect of scholarly responsibility. It is both unfair and unwise for a translator to appear to have the final word on all exegetical matters, especially when in many instances alternative interpretations are almost equally valid.

At the same time, it is unrealistic and misleading to the average reader to introduce all the alternative interpretations that have been advocated by various scholars throughout the years. This would produce a set of marginal notes fully as long as the biblical text. One must select the important differences, and for the Bible as a whole these will amount to some three or four hundred passages.

In dealing with misleading or meaningless historical or cultural events, one can either supply a marginal note to explain the relevance of the event, or in some instances provide in the text itself an identifying expression, which may be combined with the original literal expression to form what may be called a "semantic doublet."

For example, if anointing with oil as a symbol of appointment to a special task is entirely unknown, it may be possible in some passages to employ, as already noted, a phrase such as "to appoint by pouring oil on his head." The addition of "to appoint" serves as a generic expression to identify the function of the otherwise misleading reference to anointing. In a number of contexts, however, the action of anointing may be entirely secondary to the function of appointing and accordingly a verb meaning "to appoint to a task" may be sufficient.

Any generic expression of function should consist in a short, succinct expression. A long, involved explanation would be anachronistic, for it would suggest that the original author himself was required to provide built-in explanations of what should have been entirely obvious to his readers.

In some areas of West Africa the action of putting branches in the path of an oncoming chief or high official is equivalent to serious insult, and hence the action of the crowd placing branches in the path of Jesus as he rode into Jerusalem would be seriously misunderstood unless the Scriptures have some explanation, either in the text or the margin. It would be possible to identify the significance of the event by placing in the text a generic qualifier—for example, "in order to honor Jesus they placed branches in his path." This could then be followed by a fuller explanation in the margin.

Similarly, the surprise of the disciples at the fact that Jesus was talking with the Samaritan woman, when rabbis were not supposed to talk to women, might be indicated in the form of the question, "Why are you, as a rabbi, talking with her?" A fuller explanation could then be added in the margin. And in this same account the request of Jesus for a drink of water, which in some African contexts is interpreted as a request for sexual relations, could be made less open to misinterpretation by a statement in the text, "Being thirsty, Jesus said to her, 'Give me a drink of water.' "

When historical events are referred to by idiomatic expressions, one is justified in treating such idioms in the same manner as any figurative expression. For example, in Luke 13:1 the statement "whose blood Pilate mingled with their sacrifices" may be understood by some persons to imply that Pilate took some sadistic delight in mixing the blood of his human victims with the blood of the animals that had been sacrificed. The meaning, of course, is that Pilate ordered the killing of the human victims while they were sacrificing, and this nonfigurative substitute may be employed in the text of a translation.

In some instances illustrative events or states pose even greater difficulty for the translator than actual events. Some of the events or states may be relatively simple—for example, the statement in Genesis 49:12, which speaks of Judah as a person whose "eyes are bloodshot from drinking wine, and whose teeth are white from drinking milk" (although it is also possible to understand the Hebrew as meaning "his eyes are darker than wine and his teeth are whiter than milk"). But the point of such a statement is not to condemn Judah for being a drunkard or a glutton, but to emphasize his prosperity and therefore the possibility of his having plenty of wine and milk to drink. This aspect of the meaning may be indicated in the text by introducing a phrase such as "as a result of his prosperity." This same expression fits the content of the preceding verse as well.

In some cases an illustrative event may be very complex, as in the statement about the woman who was married to seven brothers, all of whom died (Matt. 22:25-28). The question posed by the Sadducees was perfectly sensible in the biblical setting, but in many parts of Africa the question about whose wife this woman is to be in the resurrection would be incredible, for any woman who seemingly caused the death of seven husbands would undoubtedly be a witch and no former husband would ever want to have anything to do with her. It is, of course, quite impossible to recast this illustrative event, but one can provide some supplementary information so that the point of Jesus' response is not lost in the amazement that some might have about the apparently preposterous question of the Sadducees.

Figurative expressions produce a number of serious problems of adjustment, but when a figurative expression can be retained, it should be. It is often possible, for example, to speak of "honoring with the lips," and one can frequently speak of "loving with the heart." In many languages, however, some slight shift in the figurative expression must be employed, and as long as the corresponding terms are within the same general domain, there is normally no difficulty involved in making a shift—for example, "honoring with the tongue" or "loving with the liver." Adjustments may also involve considerably more extensive substitutions of figurative expressions. For example, in place of "hard heart" (which in the Bible refers to stubbornness) one may have "closed ears" to express the same psychological attitude.

In a number of instances metaphors must be altered to similes. For example, in place of "I am the bread of life" (John 6:35), it may be better to say, "I am like bread that causes people to live."

When there is no related figurative expression and when a simile is not possible, it may be necessary to employ a nonfigurative expression. "Honoring with the lips" may be rendered as "honoring by what they say." When "blood" is used in a strictly figurative sense of "death," as in the expression "his blood be upon us" (Matt. 26:26), it is usually necessary to employ a nonfigurative equivalent—for example, "we will be responsible for his death." In some contexts, however, the term "blood," referring to the blood of Jesus in such contexts as Acts 20:28, Romans 3:25, and Ephesians 2:13, points not only to the death of Jesus but also to the sacrificial nature of his death. Therefore, a phrase such as "deliverance through his blood" (Eph. 1:7) may be rendered accurately as "delivered by his sacrificial death" or "delivered by his dying as a sacrifice."

When the closest corresponding objects in the source and receptor languages differ in form or function, a whole series of textual adjustments may be necessary and certain supplementary explanations may be required, either in the margin of the text or in an index or glossary.

When substantially the same types of objects occur in two different cultures but the function of such objects is quite different, it may be essential to make some adjustment in terminology. For example, many stools in West Africa have very much the same form as footstools had in the biblical culture, but in West Africa these stools are something to sit on and not a place for one's feet. In fact the king's stool has somewhat the same function in several West African societies as a scepter had in biblical culture. Because the function of the respective objects is so different, it is important to make some adjustment in speaking about a footstool in the Bible. Often this can be done by using a generic descriptive phrase, "something to put one's feet on," but in other instances it may be useful to use a different object that has essentially the same function—for example, "footboard" or "footstick," often used as a means of keeping one's feet off a damp cold floor.

Corresponding types of adjustments are required when the source and receptor cultures have objects that are substantially different in form, but have essentially the same function. For example, the stones used by Indians in Latin America for grinding grain are quite different in shape and size from those used for grinding in biblical times, but the function is sufficiently similar to permit the substitution of the Latin American *metate* for the biblical millstone. Similarly, the sword of the Bible and the *machete* of Latin America or the panga-knife of Africa are somewhat different in form, but they can be used for stabbing and killing and therefore one may be substituted for the other, especially inasmuch as they belong to essentially the same domain of artifacts.

When there are no closely resembling objects having correspondingly related functions, it may be possible to employ descriptive phrases consisting of a rather high-level generic term (a type of classifier or identifier) combined with a phrase that describes the form or states the function. For example, in areas where wolves are unknown, some translators have used a phrase "fierce wild dog" or "fierce dog-like animal." The reference to "dog" or "animal" provides a kind of generic classifier and "fierce" or "fierce wild" indicates an essential and distinguishing characteristic.

In some languages there is simply no term for "God," in the sense of a spirit being who has created the world or some part of it or who has jurisdiction over some aspect of creation. It is, however, appropriate in many languages to speak of God as "Spirit," and one may add to this some distinctive characteristic such as "eternal" (with a resulting phrase "Eternal Spirit") or a distinctive function such as "creator" (with a resulting phrase "Creator Spirit").

Few languages have an equivalent for the biblical denarius and because currencies fluctuate so much, it is inadvisable to employ local monetary units, whether based on silver content or even on presumed buying power. It may, however, be useful to follow the example of a number of translations that define the denarius in terms of "a coin equal to a day's wage."

When there are no objects in the source and receptor cultures that are similar either in form or function, it may be necessary to resort to borrowing. This is almost always done in the case of such proper names as Pharisees and Sadducees, though the reference carried by these terms needs to be explained in a glossary.

In borrowing, however, there are some serious problems, as already noted: (1) the necessity of filling such terms with proper semantic content and (2) the need to make certain that the borrowed term is not identical with or very similar to an already existing word in the language, for such a situation is likely to give rise to serious confusion. For every newly borrowed term or phrase there must be some adequate explanation in a glossary, and all important borrowed proper names should be identified in an index.

A few translators have felt that nothing should be introduced into a translation that is not already fully understandable and used in the receptor language. But such a principle is almost equivalent to saying that one can never say anything in a language that has not been heard before. Language, however, is precisely the kind of code that makes possible the communication of concepts that are new to a people, and one must not rule out concepts merely because they are not already in use. In fact the whole point of Bible translating is to tell persons the Good News—which is new!

One translator insisted on dropping the figurative use of life and death in various passages because, he contended, the receptor people did not employ these concepts in any relation to the new kind of life in Christ Jesus. But the numerous occurrences of the theme of life and death are so integral a part of the biblical message that one simply cannot avoid their use. To omit them from a translation not only does violence to the integrity of the text but deprives the receptors of important truths vital to the Christian message.

Whenever the interpretation of a passage is dependent upon some other passage or whenever readers may be materially assisted in understanding one text by having another text called to their attention, the appropriate cross-referencing should be employed. Similarly, there should be references to all (1) parallel passages (such references can be most conveniently placed immediately after section headings), (2) quotations, and (3) passages treating the same theme in a related manner, in which case the references may be given on the page of the text or by means of an index or concordance.

Notes and Textual Adjustments Not Admissible in Bible Translations Published by the United Bible Societies

In order to understand more precisely what types of supplementary information are legitimate in translations of the Bible published by the Bible Societies, it may also be relevant to indicate the four major types of notes and textual adjustments that are not admissible:

1. Notes that are dogmatic, doctrinal, or homiletical, whether inserted into the text or as supplementary to the text. All such information is perfectly legitimate in commentaries, but should not be regarded as a part of or a normal complement of a Bible Society publication.

2. Supplementary information that is extensive and involved. In one instance, an introduction to Philemon turned out to be twice as long as the text itself. For the most part, supplementary information on cultural and historical nonconformities (i.e., between source and receptor texts) should

not consist of more than two or three sentences. Supplementary information should be clear and brief.

3. Radical transpositions of major sections of the text, either for reasons of
style or presumed historical sources. Such reordering of the text is not
advisable, because such changes usually violate the integrity of the original
communication and they almost inevitably result in distortions of the
meaning.

4. Supplementary information in the text that is not specifically justified by
the syntactic or semantic structures. Such supplementary information
may, of course, be added in the margin, a glossary, or introduction.

Location of Supplementary Information

There is a tendency to think of supplementary information only in terms of
marginal notes on the page with the text. In reality, there are a number of
types of supplementary information that can best be presented at different
places:

1. *Section headings.* Section headings should immediately precede the material to which they refer and which they help to identify. They are always in a
different style and size of type, so as not to be confused with the text itself.
Such headings should not be explanatory but identificational, and insofar as
possible the vocabulary for such section headings should be drawn from the
text to which the heading refers.

2. *Cross-references.* Cross-references occur normally in three different
places: (1) immediately below the section heading, if the reference is to a
parallel passage; (2) at the foot of the page, if the reference is to a quotation
or passage that treats the same subject in an extensive or highly significant
manner; and (3) in an index or concordance, appended to the volume.

3. *Marginal notes.* Marginal notes that are important to explain historical
and cultural differences with respect to specific events should be placed at the
foot of the same page as the passage to which they refer, rather than gathered
together in an appendix. It is also useful to have marginal notes for alternative readings and renderings (i.e., variant texts and different interpretations)
on the same page with the biblical texts to which they are related, but such
notes may also be gathered together in lists in an appendix.

4. *Identification or explanation of frequently recurring objects or events.*
Notes that are necessary to identify or explain frequently recurring objects or
events—for example, the meaning of zero terms and technical vocabulary—
should appear in a glossary, index, concordance, tables (e.g., weights and
measures), or maps. It may be useful in some cases (especially in initial publications) to star those terms that occur in a glossary, but if the glossary is
properly prepared for the intended audience, it will no doubt contain most, if
not all, the words that the average reader is likely to want to look up. A

glossary is the natural place for the explanation of the meaning of zero terms, technical vocabulary, or unusual practices described in the Bible.

In some instances it may be useful to combine certain features of a glossary and index, so that the index itself will contain identifications of meaning. Similarly, a brief concordance may combine certain explanatory features that are normally associated with a glossary. Weights and measures may be explained in a glossary, but it may be more convenient to treat them in a separate table. Maps should be accompanied by some key, to identify the map and area of the map where geographical names are to be found.

5. *Table of contents*. The usual table of contents for a New Testament or Bible consists simply in a listing of the various books involved. For many readers this is not particularly useful, and hence an index is almost indispensable if the reader is to find where particular subjects are treated.

6. *Index*. For a New Testament or a Bible an index is essential, for readers need to be able to find those pages on which various persons, events, and topics are discussed. An index is especially useful in distinguishing different persons who may bear the same name, in listing various parables, discourses, events, and miracles, and in identifying those passages in which certain important themes (e.g., love, grace, redemption, salvation, and repentance) are dealt with.

7. *Introductions*. An introduction should ideally contain information about the author, the place and time of writing, the intended audience, and the principal themes of the book. But not all this type of information is available for most of the books of the Bible, and it is neither helpful nor wise to include in an introduction merely a discussion of various scholarly viewpoints concerning issues of authorship and dating. Accordingly, the introductions that are being prepared for use in publications of the United Bible Societies contain primarily (1) a statement of the important theme or themes, (2) the significance of the book, in terms of its original setting, and (3) the relevance of the message of the book for the present-day reader. Certain adjustments are obviously necessary in the case of special audiences.

The Form of Marginal Notes

Marginal notes have several different forms, depending upon the subject matter being discussed. Notes regarding alternative readings (i.e., variant forms of the text) may contain such introductory expressions as "other ancient manuscripts have . . ." or "some ancient manuscripts add. . . ." It is usually not wise to attempt an evaluation of the evidence in a translation designed for a general audience, because details of manuscript sources may be more misleading than helpful. On the other hand, it is important to have some expression for "manuscripts"—for example, "some old copies written by hand" or "some many-generations-old handwritten editions of the Holy Writings." Some translators have endeavored to employ simply "some old Bibles," but this may appear to be only a reference to old dilapidated volumes of printed Bibles. The value of some reference to manuscripts is to provide some basis for later explanations of how easily some mistakes can arise when materials are copied by hand, with copyists looking back and forth from text to copy.

Because in many instances marginal notes have to deal with additions that are typical of the fuller text of the Textus Receptus tradition, it may be useful merely to employ half-brackets (the lower half of square brackets) to enclose such words and to have an introductory statement on the back of the title page or in a preface indicating that words enclosed in such half-brackets do not occur in some of the oldest and best manuscripts.

In the case of alternative interpretations one can introduce the variant rendering simply by "Or . . . ." When the alternative renderings are gathered together in a list, it may be useful to have a brief introductory statement, "In the case of the following passages, it is also possible to interpret the Greek (or Hebrew, as the case may be) in a somewhat different manner from what has been given in the text of the translation. . . ." It is generally unwise and unnecessary to attempt detailed explanations of why there are such differences of interpretation. The average reader is only interested in the results of scholarly opinion, not in the manner in which one has arrived at such conclusions.

Marginal notes that deal with supplementary information necessary for the proper comprehension of the text are for the most part of two types: (1) identificational and (2) explanatory. Identificational notes are essentially definitions, according to the formula: "A is a B, with the features of C"—in which A is the term being identified or defined, B is a generic substitute for this term, and C are the specific attributes that help to distinguish A from all the other objects or events that might be classified as B.

For example, in the descriptive definition of Pharisees, one may state, "The Pharisees were a Jewish religious party (or sect), which insisted upon strict observance of the Old Testament law and the traditions associated with it." The term "Pharisees" is item A, and "religious party" is B (a highly generic expression). The qualifications "Jewish" and the postposed clause "which insisted . . . with it" are the C elements. This definition does not include all that is known about the Pharisees, and for such supplementary information one may include a number of biblical references (e.g., Matt. 5:20, 16:6, 23:13-27; Acts 23:6-9).

In general, it is not necessary or expedient to put too much information in an identificational note. All that is required is that the reader be able to understand the principal characteristics or features.

Similarly, one may have a note on "camel," saying, "The camel is a large domesticated animal, used for the transport of people and goods, especially in desert areas." In this descriptive definition "camel" is item A, the term "animal" is B, and the qualifications "large," "domesticated," and "used for transport . . . in desert areas" help to distinguish this animal from such other animals as the hippopotamus (which is not domesticated), sheep (which is not large), and horse (which is not used primarily in desert areas). It would also be possible to speak of camels as having large humps that serve for storage of water, but it would be even better to have a picture of camels being ridden or carrying loads.

In a number of cases the functional value of some object may be much more important than its size or shape. For example, the denarius contained silver equivalent to approximately 35 cents U.S., but its buying power was much greater, being the average day's wage for a common laborer. Accordingly, it is much better to define a denarius as "a coin that was equivalent to a day's wage of a common laborer," rather than to give some equivalence in grams of silver or corresponding present-day value of the metal.

Marginal notes that treat cultural and historical differences must be considerably more complex than those that are merely identificational. In general, they should contain the following information: (1) an indication of the significance or meaning of the biblical object or event, in terms of the existing presuppositions and value system, (2) a denial of the validity of interpreting the event or object in terms of the receptor viewpoint, and (3) the identification of some equivalent event or object in the receptor culture.

For example, as already noted, in the case of a translation for a language in West Africa in which the account of the putting of branches in Jesus' path as he went into Jerusalem would be seriously misunderstood, an appropriate note of the following type is crucial: "In the time of Jesus, placing branches in the path of an oncoming chief or ruler was a way of showing him honor. It did not mean that he was being dishonored. This placing of branches in Jesus' path would be equivalent to the way in which many people in Africa sweep the path when a dignitary is coming to visit." When a biblical event or object has an entirely different or contrary meaning to what it has in the receptor culture, it is often useful to state this fact both positively ("was a way of showing him honor") and negatively ("it did not mean that he was being dishonored"). Following this positive and negative statement of the biblical feature, one can then mention a local equivalent custom.

Implications of Marginal Helps in Scriptures Published by the United Bible Societies

One may very well question how it is that the United Bible Societies encourage the introduction of marginal helps, when traditionally they have been known to insist on publishing the Scriptures "without note or comment." A brief consideration of the traditional position of the Bible Societies may therefore be useful in understanding what is actually involved.

In order to encourage the widest possible distribution and acceptance of the Scriptures, the Bible Societies have attempted to avoid interconfessional conflicts by publishing Bibles without notes, especially in the major European languages. But the Bible Societies have never ceased to publish Bibles with *certain types* of notes and marginal helps, because the phrase "without note and comment" has always been interpreted as referring to doctrinal and dogmatic notes. This is fully understandable, inasmuch as it was over doctrinal and dogmatic notes that the early controversies arose.

The Bible Societies have continued to provide Scriptures with alternative readings and renderings, with reference systems, and often with chapter summaries and running heads. In areas where particular historical and cultural features of the Bible might lead to misunderstanding, as for example in many parts of the Orient, the Bible Societies did not hesitate to supply a limited number of marginal aids designed to help readers understand the meaning of the text and the cultural significance of the events. Hence, what is now being done and advocated by the Bible Societies is not so radical a departure as it might seem.

At the present time there is a new dimension in Scripture distribution and use that makes it imperative that more supplementary helps be made available to the average reader. The Bible is no longer being supplied merely or primarily to church members. It is increasingly being bought and read by non-Christians who have little or no access to necessary supplementary information. Accordingly, representatives of the churches, and especially of those churches that are most active in the use and distribution of the Scriptures (in most instances this means the more theologically conservative constituencies), are insisting that the New Testament and the Bible must be produced with adequate supplementary helps.

At the same time, leaders of the Roman Catholic Church have recognized the value and wisdom of cooperation with Protestants in the translation, publication, and distribution of the Scriptures. And they have recognized that the types of marginal helps being provided by the United Bible Societies are essentially those that Roman Catholics also need.

Therefore, in line with precisely these new developments and on the basis of their long tradition, the Bible Societies are encouraging and even insisting upon the incorporation of adequate supplementary helps, designed to make the Scriptures more useful and meaningful, while at the same time guarding against unwarranted linguistic and cultural "transpositions" and "reinterpretations" of the message.

Appendix

As translators or others read this volume they may wonder about types of problems found in others parts of the Scriptures. It may be useful, therefore, to follow up the implications of certain principles by analyzing and discussing a number of relatively different expressions that occur in the Bible. These are listed in classified form here and may be particularly helpful to translators who wish to investigate some of the implications suggested by the principles set forth in this book. The order of the various sets of problems involving equivalences roughly parallels the topics discussed in the various chapters.

1. Certain terms used in everyday language take on a different meaning in their biblical contexts. Compare the meanings of *peace, law, inherit,* and *hope* in the following expressions:
   the God of peace *vs.* they signed the peace treaty.
   the law of Moses *vs.* the law of the land
   inherit the kingdom of God *vs.* he inherited his father's estate.
   faith, hope, and love *vs.* I hope to see you soon.

2. Compare the expression "I tore my shirt" with the cultural implication in 2 Samuel 1:11, "David tore his clothes." The same customary behavior is used by the high priest in Mark 14:63 with a different motivation.

3. Certain events may appear to be irrelevant to their contexts and consequently are often overlooked or wrongly interpreted:
   Jesus sitting down to teach (Matt. 5:1–2)
   healing after sundown (Mark 1:32)
   Jesus conversing with a woman (John 4)
   Jesus going through Samaria (John 4:4)

4. Indicate the cultural patterns implied in the somewhat obscure reference "in the gate."

5. Casting of lots, allowing the hair to go uncut (in the Nazarite vows), and the levirate marriage are patterns of behavior, the validity of which is open to divergent judgment. List some others.

6. In the following beliefs indicate those that are biblical, involving in some cases differences between Old Testament and New Testament views:
   a. *History*
      1. cyclic view
      2. inevitable progress

      3. rise and fall
      4. Kingdom of heaven
  b. *Destiny of persons*
      1. heaven or hell
      2. heaven
      3. no future life
      4. murky, shadowy existence
  c. *Supernatural beings*
      1. one God
      2. one God superior to other gods
      3. spirits but no gods
      4. no gods or spirits
  d. *Human nature*
      1. basically evil
      2. basically good
      3. good or bad depending on environment
      4. capacity for improvement
  e. *Nature of human persons*
      1. basically physical
      2. body and mind
      3. body, soul, and spirit
      4. spiritual nature trapped in body

7. What cultural assumptions underlie the following unusual events?
  a. Jacob wrestled with a supernatural being at the Jabbok and demanded his name (Gen. 32).
  b. David took a census of Israel and Judah and a punishment resulted (2 Sam. 24).
  c. Absalom pitched a tent on David's roof in Jerusalem and had relations with the royal concubines (2 Sam. 16).
  d. Uriah the Hittite did not go home to his wife when he returned from the battle (2 Sam. 11).
  e. "And the servants of the King of Syria said to him, 'Their gods are gods of the hills . . . let us fight them in the plain' " (1 Kings 1:50).
  f. Jesus healed a woman who had been bound for eighteen years (Luke 13).
  g. The Jewish officials led Jesus from the house of Caiaphas to the praetorium but did not enter it, for they wished to eat the passover (John 18:28).
  h. The apostles selected Judas' replacement by casting lots (Acts 1).

8. Underlying the following events are certain beliefs or attitudes. Do people today approve or disapprove of these?
  a. commandment against eating flesh that is torn by beasts in the field (Exod. 22:31)
  b. holy war (Deut. 13:2–5; 1 Sam. 15:3; Josh. 6:18)

    c. circumcision (Gen. 17; Luke 1:59)

    d. blessing (Gen. 27; Deut. 6:7)

    e. cursing (Exod. 21:17; Deut. 27:15–26)

    f. sacred places (1 Kings 14:23; Gen. 12; Deut. 16:21)

    g. sacrifice (Lev. 1)

    h. ordeal (Exod. 32:20)

    i. fasting (2 Sam. 12:15–23; Mark 2:18)

9. What kind of marginal note would be required for the items in No. 8 in an English translation designed for high school students?

10. Determine the differences of underlying beliefs relating to the following subjects in the Old Testament and in certain New Testament passages:

    a. God in the council of the gods in the Old Testament, and gods in the New Testament

    b. sheol and heaven

    c. polygamy

    d. circumcision

11. Examine the following terms and expressions and indicate those that are figurative and those that are specific historical events:

    a. wineskins (Mark 2:22)

    b. yoke (Matt. 11:29; 1 Kings 12:4)

    c. sacrifice (Ps. 51:17; Gen. 8:20)

    d. shepherd (Ps. 23; Amos 1:1)

    e. adultery (Jer. 3:9)

    f. crown (Song of Sol. 3:11; Heb. 2:9)

    g. sheep (Jer. 50:17; Gen.3 12:16)

12. Examine the following terms and expressions and determine if they are important in terms of religious significance or have relatively little religious significance:

    a. coat (Matt. 5:40)

    b. camel (Matt. 19:24)

    c. vineyard (Mark 12)

    d. beating the breast (Luke 18:13)

    e. cross (Matt. 10:38)

    f. temple (Mark 14:58)

    g. sacrifice (Gen. 31:54)

    h. kingdom (Matt. 12:25)

    i. the cup of his wrath (Isa. 51:17)

    j. sons of the resurrection (Luke 20:36)

    k. right hand of the power of God (Luke 22:69)

13. Examine the possible degrees of religious significance in the following passages involving "cup" and "sheep": Ps. 11:6, 16:5, 23:5, 75:8, 116:13; Is. 51:17, 53:7; Jer. 16:7, 50:6; Ezek. 34:11–12; Matt. 10:6, 25:32; Luke 15:6; John 10:2, 21:17; 1 Cor. 10:16; Rev. 14:10

14. What kind of marginal note would be required to explain the significance of the following concepts or events?
    a. blood vengeance
    b. cities of refuge
    c. kinship obligations of the *go'el*
    d. taboo on women during menstruation

15. What are the meanings of the following expressions and what are the customs that provide a basis for such meanings?
    a. cover his feet (Judg. 3:24)
    b. born upon Joseph's knees (Gen. 50:23)

16. Formulate explanatory marginal notes for the following events and indicate two or three biblical references to assist the reader:
    a. adoption
    b. alms giving
    c. anoint
    d. covenant
    e. birthright
    f. purification following birth
    g. swearing an oath

Selected Bibliography

Aland, Kurt, and others (eds.) 1966 *The Greek New Testament* New York and London: United Bible Societies

Benedict, Ruth 1946 *The Chrysanthemum and the Sword* Boston: Houghton and Mifflin

Brower, Reuben A. (ed.) 1959 *On Translation* Cambridge: Harvard University Press

Cary, E. and R. W. Jumpelt (eds.) 1963 *Quality in Translation* New York: Macmillan

Cherry, Colin 1957 *On Human Communication* Cambridge: The M.I.T. Press

Colby, B. N. 1966 Cultural patterns in narrative *Science* 151.793-798

de Vaux, Roland 1961 *Ancient Israel: Its Life and Institutions* London: Darton, Longman and Todd

Doneux, J. L. 1969 L'Afrique entre la tradition orale et la rationalite scientifique *Afrique et Parole* 27.3-17

Gerard, R., C. Kluckhohn and A. Rapaport 1956 Biological and cultural evolution: some analogies and explorations *Behavioral Science* 1.6-34

Goldschmidt, Walter 1977 Anthropology and the coming crisis: an autoethnographic appraisal *American Anthropologist* 79.293-308

Güttinger, Fritz 1963 *Zielsprache: Theorie und Technik des Überstezens* Zürich: Manesse Verlag

Hall, E. T. and George Trager 1953 *The Analysis of Culture* Washington: American Council of Learned Societies

Halliday, M. A. K., Angus McIntosh, and Peter Strevens 1964 *The Users and Uses of Language* London: Longman

Hockett, C. F. 1977 *The View from Language: Selected Essays 1948-1974* Athens, Georgia: University of Georgia Press

Hymes, Dell (ed.) 1964 *Language in Culture and Society: a Reader in Linguistics and Anthropology* New York: Harper and Row

Knox, Ronald 1949 *Trials of a Translator* New York: Sheed and Ward

Lambert, Wallace E., Howard Giles, and Omer Picard 1975 Language attitudes in a French-American community *Linguistics* 158.127-152

Masters, Roger D. 1970 Genes, language, and evolution *Semiotica* 4.295-320

Miller, George A., E. Galanter, and K. Pribram 1960 *Plans and the Structure of Behavior* New York: Holt, Rinehart, and Winston

Nida, Eugene A. 1954 *Customs and Cultures* New York: Harper and Row (now published by William Carey Library)

—— 1960 *Message and Mission* New York: Harper and Row (now published by William Carey Library)

—— 1964 *Toward A Science of Translating* Leiden, The Netherlands: E. J. Brill

—— 1968 *Religion Across Cultures* New York: Harper and Row

—— Charles R. Taber 1969 *The Theory and Practice of Translation* Leiden, The Netherlands: E. J. Brill

—— 1974 *Understanding Latin Americans* Pasadena, California: William Carey Library

—— 1975 *Exploring Semantic Structures* Münich: Wilhelm Fink Verlag

—— 1975 *Componential Analysis of Meaning* The Hague: Mouton

——— 1975 *Language Structure and Translation* Stanford, California: Stanford University Press

Poyatos, Fernando 1972 The communication system of the speaker-actor and his culture *Linguistics* 83.64–86

Read, Kenneth E. 1965 *The High Valley* New York: Charles Scribner's Sons

Sebeok, Thomas A. (ed.) 1960 *Style in Language* New York: Wiley M. I. T. Press

Sturtevant, William C. 1964 Studies in Ethnoscience *American Anthropologist* 66.299–131

Tyler, Stephen A. (ed.) 1969 *Cognitive Anthropology* New York: Holt, Rinehart, and Winston

Weinreich, Uriel 1953 *Languages in Contact* New York: Linguistic Circle of New York

Whiteley, W. H. (ed.) 1971 *Language Use and Social Change* Oxford: University Press

Wilden, Anthony 1972 Analog and digital communication *Semiotica* 6.50–82

Biblical Index

General Index

7022